Items should be returned on or before the last date shown below. Items not already requested by other borrowers may be renewed in person, in writing or by telephone. To renew, please quote the number on the barcode label. To renew online a PIN is required. This can be requested at your local library.

Renew online @ **www.dublincitypubliclibraries.ie**

Fines charged for overdue items will include postage incurred in recovery. Damage to or loss of items will be charged to the borrower.

Leabharlanna Poiblí Chathair Bhaile Átha Cliath
Dublin City Public Libraries

Baile Átha Cliath
Dublin City

Brainse Rátheanaigh
Raheny Branch
Tel: 8315521

Date Due	Date Due	Date Due
0/9/2016		
08/06		
24 FEB 2018		

R
Fi
inc
be

Le

THE

Ian Fleming

MISCELLANY

THE

Ian Fleming

MISCELLANY

ANDREW COOK

For Alia

First published 2015

The History Press
The Mill, Brimscombe Port
Stroud, Gloucestershire, GL5 2QG
www.thehistorypress.co.uk

© Andrew Cook, 2015

The right of Andrew Cook to be identified as
the Author of this work has been asserted in accordance
with the Copyrights, Designs and Patents Act 1988.

British Library Cataloguing in Publication Data.
A catalogue record for this book is available from the British Library.

ISBN 978 0 7509 6091 5

Typesetting and origination by The History Press
Printed in Great Britain by TJ International Ltd, Padstow, Cornwall

CONTENTS

• 1 •
Silver Spoon   7
• 2 •
The Trouble with Women   25
• 3 •
There Will be War   37
• 4 •
The Dream Job   49
• 5 •
Meticulous Plotting   63
• 6 •
More War   85
• 7 •
Jamaica   97
• 8 •
Shotgun   115

• 9 •
Technique   *131*
• 10 •
Love and Marriage   *155*
• 11 •
The Big Mistake   *167*
• 12 •
The Killer   *179*

List of Abbreviations   *191*

SILVER SPOON

· THE END IN THE BEGINNING ·

Ian Fleming's birth and upbringing nurtured the talent, urbanity and focus that made him successful, but also the arrogance and self-doubt that caught up with him in the end.

He was born into a family of great wealth and extraordinary talent. Only two generations back, his paternal great-grandfather had been a humble Dundee bookkeeper. His grandfather had begun work at 13, learned how to invest other people's money and founded his eponymous merchant bank Robert Fleming and Co. before he was 30. Having left Scotland for New York, he made influential friends, among them the international banking magnates John Pierpoint Morgan and Jacob Schiff.

In the early twentieth century his bank changed its base from Dundee to the City of London, and Robert and his wife, Kathleen, moved the family to a mansion in Grosvenor Square.

The older of Robert Fleming's two sons was Valentine, known as Val. On Val's marriage to Eve Ste Croix Rose, Robert gave the couple £250,000 – tens of millions today. Val became a barrister, and MP for Henley, and had four sons of his own: Peter, Ian, Richard and Michael, in that order. Their mother, Eve, was a pretty and sociable woman of distinguished heritage and with a strong sense of entitlement.

Perhaps it was all too perfect to last. Valentine Fleming served in the First World War as a major in the Queen's Own Oxfordshire Hussars and was killed in Picardy in 1917. His closest friend, who appreciated him as a kind and honourable man and wrote a sad and loving obituary in *The Times*, was Winston Churchill. Valentine left money in trust for his sons and their education. For Eve, there was an extremely generous allowance for life unless she remarried, in which case her stipend would be considerably reduced.

All the boys boarded at a prep school – which Ian hated – before taking up places at Eton. They were close, especially Ian and his older brother Peter, who remembered their father well and understood the terrible finality of his death when it happened. At Eton, Peter took the academic prizes while Ian concentrated on establishing his physical prowess. 'Victor Ludorum twice,' he said proudly to Roy Plomley, when asked about Eton decades later in a BBC radio interview. He also edited a school magazine, wrote poetry and made dozens of friends for life. There were escapades with Ivar Bryce, a rich, young fellow pupil. Together they discovered motorbikes, fast cars and the thrill of escape from authority.

Eve Fleming, meanwhile, indulged a penchant for Upper Bohemia. Ian had been born in Green Street, Mayfair, but for most of his childhood the family had occupied Pitt House at North End, Hampstead. This was the home Eve had shared with her husband and where she entertained a large circle of friends. In 1923, she sold it and moved to the unfashionable, least accessible part of Chelsea: a row of unassuming cottages at the west end of Cheyne Walk. One of them was distinguished by having been home to J.M.W. Turner. She bought it, and the two others either side of it, and got the builders in; she ended up with a twelve-bedroomed mansion with a lot of space for grand gatherings of well-off and slightly louche musicians, artists and writers. She was a pretty widow; Augustus John, who, at 45, was seven years older, lived with the mother of some of his many children. He was a notorious philanderer. His studio was nearby, across the King's Road in Mallord Street. The inevitable happened – or, quite possibly, it had already happened, for a move from sturdy, family friendly Hampstead to what was then arty, edgy Chelsea seems otherwise unlikely.

Quite how much Eve's oldest sons knew of her affair with Augustus John is uncertain. In 1925, at 17, he wrote a story in *Wyvern*, an Eton College magazine, and the thread that ran through it was the infidelity of women. Was he secretly hurt and censorious about his mother's 'betrayal' of his deceased father? We cannot know. Like most teenagers, Ian was probably self-obsessed and not much interested. He would soon follow his brother into adult life, which meant making his mark, somehow. Eton encouraged its pupils to think of themselves as leaders of men.

Peter, the eldest of the four, was tough-minded. He refused to countenance a career in the family bank and devoted himself to becoming a writer. His mother encouraged him, and his success at Eton led to Christ Church, Oxford, and a First in English.

Ian, as the second son, lived in Peter's shadow. As a student, he was careless. As an athlete, he excelled. He was not a great team player, but he liked challenging games such as golf and even bridge, and he was by no means stupid. At 18 he seemed to be imaginative and outgoing but lazy. What to do about Ian? His house-master, Edward Vere Slater, MA Oxon, co-author of a popular Latin Grammar, judged grimly that Fleming Minor 'could do better' and, regarding the boy's academic failure as inevitable, recommended a term in a crammer as preparation for officer training at Sandhurst.

• TRYING HARD •

Later in life Ian said he'd wanted, at the time, to go into the Black Watch. He took his Scottish ancestry seriously. But he was unsuited to regimentation, and he faded away from Sandhurst after a year – with gonorrhoea, according to a biographer, contracted after a brief encounter with a girl at the 43, Mrs Meyrick's notorious nightclub in Gerrard Street. Nearly twenty years would pass before antibiotics became generally available and until then there was no reliable treatment for venereal disease.

Plan B, in 1927, was more successful. 'I had a go at the Diplomatic,' drawled Ian on the radio in 1963. This meant the Diplomatic Service of the Foreign Office, which required fluency in languages – an excuse to go abroad.

As his exasperated mother knew, not only had he caught the clap but he had done so when in keen pursuit of another girl for whom he was still pining. Abroad was definitely a good idea.

She made enquiries and pulled strings, something she would do again and again until Ian found his niche. She despatched him to Kitzbühel in Austria, where an interesting couple called Forbes Dennis ran a school. Ian found an enchanting Tyrolean town with winding mediaeval streets and snowy mountains where he could learn to ski well. A.E. Forbes Dennis had been the British Passport Control Officer at the Vienna Embassy – that is, in charge of British intelligence for Austria and the lands around it. Nigel West traces Fleming's aspiration to improve his German and French, join the Foreign Office and get into intelligence, to Forbes Dennis. Mrs Forbes Dennis, better known as Phyllis Bottome, was a novelist and biographer.

He enjoyed himself. Not only did he make friends of both sexes, drive fast and expertly, and feel freer than he had in England, but he may have received a grounding in popular writing from Phyllis Bottome, who respected his talents. He was already an avid reader of adventure stories, but from her he could learn how to plunge right in, set a scene and introduce characters and the relationship between them in the first few pages. She was not aiming at literary fiction and deployed predictable techniques. In her stories, which can be over-reliant on expository dialogue, key characters make a memorable entrance and one colourful location follows another as in the scenes of a play. There's conflict, unresolved sexual tension, identifiable motive, desirable outcome and generally everything that makes people want to turn the pages.

After Kitzbühel there were courses at Munich University and the University of Geneva. Four years after leaving Sandhurst, Ian could read and speak French and German well and Russian passably. He was back in England ready to be considered, by examination and interview, for a job in the Foreign Office, and he had a serious girlfriend, Monique Panchaud de Bottomes. They became engaged in 1931. He was 23 and still living at home when he was in England. Monique came to spend a few days at Cheyne Walk, which was a disaster since his mother made it clear to him that this Swiss girl of the haute bourgeoisie was in no respect haute enough to become a Fleming (she had caught her creeping towards Ian's bedroom at night). Monique left.

Ian did not get one of the few vacancies at the Foreign Office. Until the day he died, he said he had come seventh and there were only five places. Later research has revealed that he did not get anywhere near the top of the list, and he must have been bitterly disappointed.

• INFLUENCE •

Nil desperandum. Eve was not lacking in grit and nor were the Fleming grandparents. Old Robert, now in his late 80s, and his eccentric wife, Kathleen, lived, as they had done since long before the First World War, between Grosvenor Square and a vast mock-Tudor house called Joyce Grove outside Nettlebed in Oxfordshire. Perhaps Granny Fleming's dour assessment of the prospects for a young man without a job stung Eve into action, or maybe she was already aware that London in the twenties and early thirties was over-supplied with unemployed young men qualified in the arts and classics, with oodles of charm and bags of background but no understanding of science or business. Anyhow, she set about finding work for Ian.

Her second son's interests, other than dining, drinking, girls and fast cars, were writing and travelling. She scanned her address book with a frown, flipped past Beaverbrook, ignored Rothermere and found the head of Reuters. Surely Sir Roderick Jones could do something? Indeed, he could. In October 1931, Ian joined the news agency as subeditor and journalist.

Reuters' intermittent link to the Secret Service dated back many years, but in 1916, after the death of Baron Hubert de Reuter, the company received a guaranteed subsidy from Secret Service funds to enable Sir Roderick Jones to buy it. Jones had been the Reuters South Africa correspondent during the Boer War, and when the Ministry of Information was created he became its Director of Propaganda.

Reuters was perfect for Fleming. Boring, repetitious tasks were cut to a minimum. Deadlines, witty company, drinks at El Vino's, endless novelty and the creative challenge of grabbing public attention and keeping it were just what he needed. He became, by trial and error, a newsman. He learned to write vividly, with economy and impact. He loved it, and he got paid. He left the western edge of Chelsea for a flat of his own at the eastern edge, where Belgravia began, in Ebury Street. He had a Buick, and he reported on the Alpine Motor Trials from Munich in 1932. He actually took part, with an experienced co-driver, and loved every minute of it.

The young Ian Fleming, Reuter's correspondent, as pictured in his Visa application to the Soviet authorities, 1939. *GARF*

• SEIZING THE MOMENT •

March 1933 was tense. This was the month in which Hitler slithered from coalition leader to outright dictatorship in Germany. But it was news from Moscow that electrified Parliament. Six British, and many more Russian, Metro-Vickers engineers had been arrested on charges of espionage or treason. There was an immediate call for a trade embargo.

The government's consternation arose from complacency about the assistance Britain was affording to Stalin's Five Year Plan. In the 1800s, British engineers had built railways the world over, and now, in the new century, our expertise in power generation would propel Russia's vast downtrodden populace into the twentieth century. Mr Stalin, we assumed, must be grateful.

Apparently not. The Ambassador was recalled. The men would soon be tried and sentenced. All the news agencies wanted reporters in the courtroom and every one of them would be vying to get his piece back first. Ian Fleming's editor picked him to represent Reuters alongside their resident reporter in Moscow. The least experienced foreign journalist there, he rose to the occasion. He arrived well ahead of time and began sending despatches back, building up the tension. Alone among the press pack, he travelled out of Moscow to the Vickers compound and interviewed the five engineers who were being held on bail.

When the case came to court, just one of the British men pleaded guilty. (Even he claimed later to have done so only because his Russian lady housekeeper, whom he loved, would otherwise be shot.) All the rest pleaded innocent. The outcome of their trial was impossible to guess.

'Everything depends on getting in first!' Fleming had been warned. Every other journalist knew that too, so they tried bribing the girls in the telegraph office down the road from the courthouse. Fleming decided this would never work. Instead, since every cable had to be read and passed before despatch, he made a special friend of a censor. What if, he asked his friend, he were to draft two stories with alternative outcomes, and when judgement was passed, he telephoned the cable office and the censor filled in the gaps in the right one and sent it first ..? *Niet*. So Fleming came up with another plan. He found a boy. He found running shoes that fitted the boy. He stationed the boy beneath a window outside the courtroom and disabled all the courthouse phones except one, where a *Central News* correspondent had to await a call from head office. And he sat in the courtroom, noted down the lenient sentences, added them to his prepared article, dropped the text out of the window to the running boy – and waited as the kid sprinted madly towards the telegraph office.

It should have worked. But luck was against him. The *Central News* correspondent, chewing his nails near the phone in a corridor, heard the Judge's verdict through a nearby loudspeaker, and by some fluke he got through to *Central News* in London almost immediately. They therefore obtained the result twenty minutes before Reuters did.

Moscow wasn't altogether a wasted journey. Fleming had also tried to get an interview from Stalin. He received a polite Excuse and No, personally signed, which he treasured to the end of his days. And after the trial, the foreign press contingent sent a telegram to Sir Roderick Jones, praising their new colleague Ian Fleming. 'He gave us all a run for our money' was the cheery message.

Ian had found his métier. He was offered a job in Shanghai, the most exotic town in the world and notoriously, then, the former home of Mrs Simpson. It was a dream job. He was very much tempted. But everything was about to change.

• REVISING THE PLAN •

That summer old Robert Fleming died aged 88.
His will left the huge house in Oxfordshire, No. 27
Grosvenor Square, the Scottish estate and the bulk
of his fortune to his second son, Philip. Granny
Kathleen could remain in residence at all the homes
for life. Eve would get nothing and her sons were
effectively disinherited.

They had enough, thanks to their father, to set
themselves up and would not receive enough to ruin
themselves; maybe their grandfather's will would
prove the making of all of them. But Ian knew that he
would never have the life he wanted on a journalist's
salary. Not long before, over dinner in Paris, he had
told Ivar Bryce:

He had always thought of writing as a wonderful
way of life, and again explained the advantages and
pleasures of writing thrillers while travelling about
the world. He was excited at the thought of all the
adventures and characters for plots that could be
met with in, say, Vienna, and utilised as a short-cut
to fame and fortune, with no more capital required
than a pen and a writing-pad.

That was all very well, but Ian Fleming liked dinners in Paris, and cars, and taking girls out. He needed money. His brother Peter was travelling the world and had just published *Brazilian Adventure* to loud acclaim. Peter was prepared to rough it, a condition Ian viewed with distaste. Richard and Michael, his younger brothers, had both joined Flemings and commuted happily enough into the City every day. Theirs, not Peter's, was the route to the security you needed in order – someday – to live the dreams that would – someday – come to life in best-sellers.

Ian had, by then, a lover: a sophisticated and wise older woman called Maud, who was married to Gilbert Russell, a director of Cull & Co., bankers. Gilbert was preparing to retire in a couple of years and offered Ian a job in the City. He found it congenial enough. He took people out to lunch and discussed their investments; that was about it. Socially, he spent a lot more time shooting in Scotland than he ever had before. There were games of cricket, bridge and so on. Cull & Co. paid him generously, the hours were undemanding and the seat on the board soon to be vacated would be his, so he could do pretty much as he pleased. He lived well, made friends with a knowledgeable antiquarian bookseller and began to collect rare books. And then one day in 1935 the world woke up to read in the newspapers that Cull & Co. – having made some extremely unwise investments – had lost a huge amount of money.

Gilbert Russell was asked to stay on. Ian might as well go. However, if he wished to live in the style to which he had become accustomed, he must first pass by the Labour Exchange located within the Fleming network. Through this he found a job at Rowe and Pitman, stockbrokers. It seems that some intelligence officers worked for Rowe and Pitman. Most important and well connected of all the directors was Lance Hugh Smith, whose friends included Oppenheimers, Bowes Lyons, directors of De Beers and John Pierpoint Morgan. Andrew Lycett, Fleming's biographer, read the firm's unpublished official history, and it identifies Lance Hugh Smith as a likely talent-spotter for Intelligence before, and probably during, the Second World War.

Hugh Pitman, the senior partner for whom Ian would work, was from a spectacularly well connected family himself – Hambros, a director of the National Provincial Bank, the deputy director of Naval Intelligence and many others were among them. Socially, Hugh Pitman almost certainly knew Ian's mother. He and his wife lived near Eve, and their portraits had been painted by Augustus John.

Pitman, like everyone else, could see that Ian was in the City because he knew how to spend a positively tumbling cascade of cash. Sadly, he couldn't spot a good investment if you wrapped it in red satin and pinned it to his desk. But Ian seems already to have had another agenda. When Hugh Pitman took him to New York in the autumn of 1937, Fleming seized his chance to visit Washington and talk to Alaric Jacob, his closest friend at Reuters. Jacob got the impression that Ian was unusually interested in Roosevelt's foreign policy – probably in some capacity other than stockbroking.

Certainly the business bored him. When, one night, he pleaded illness and excused himself half way through dinner with Hugh Pitman and a client, Pitman later found him in bed with a blonde at the St Regis.

Staff at Rowe and Pitman resented Ian's dismissive remarks about their business, which was making money. He might find their preoccupations mundane, but they had a gift he desperately wished to possess. He had all the advantages that a silver spoon can bestow at birth, but he wanted to prove something. He wanted to make money out of writing – and the kind of writing he wanted to do required the kind of experience he didn't yet have.

2

THE TROUBLE WITH WOMEN

· MISOGYNY ·

Boys of 8 cannot stand girls. Alarmingly, by the time Ian Fleming was a 20-something with a long trail of girlfriends, his love-hate relationship with women was still apparent. This was in part a feature of the Zeitgeist. In any man's working life women were people of no account and powerless. The glass ceiling before the Second World War rested at the level of schoolteacher, secretary or, exceptionally, head-mistress or hospital matron. *The Evening Standard* employed Stella Gibbons, author of *Cold Comfort Farm*, to write its fashion page, not its book reviews.

Socially, women – 'girls' – of his own age were prey and, by definition, foolish enough to be caught; once caught and played with, they were best despatched quickly and cleanly, with no further involvement. If they argued, they were nags. If they argued with devastating logic, they had male minds and were very probably lesbians. He was convinced of all this.

So with hindsight, Ian Fleming was a boor in this way, but his attitude was almost normal among men of his class, at least until they were over 30. Sexually attractive women were assumed to be thick as a plank.

As they aged though, women – in Ian's eyes – thought and behaved more like regular human beings (i.e. men). Circumstances such as the death of a husband, as in his mother's case, or enormous riches and great age, as in his grandmother's, could leave them in a position of power for which, in his opinion, they were likely to be unfit. Only a long life shared with intelligent men could bestow perception and empathy, and he was attracted to these qualities in older women.

In his youth, he was close to only one 'intellectual' woman, not a type he would ever have met in England. Phyllis Bottome was someone he could respect, although of course she was married, more than twice his age when he knew her and he was rather in awe of her husband. She was not prey. Nor was she authoritarian, although their relationship was that of teacher and pupil. She was liberal-minded, politically sophisticated and a prolific biographer as well as a popular novelist. Bottome had studied under Adler and was therefore aware of the latest theories about family position and its effect on one's outlook. Ian, as the second son in a family of four boys, was probably assessed as a young man with a sub-conscious drive to compensate for his relative lack of success, in order to impress his mother.

• MOTHER •

His mother was quite a piece of work. Eve was known by at least one family retainer as 'the Great I Am'. She must have been amusing within her own enormous circle of friends, but her course of action in the early 1920s, when all her sons were away at school, indicates a person unhinged. She blatantly stole another woman's baby.

Augustus John, her lover, had many illegitimate children (after Caspar and Poppet, who had been born to his wife who died). His most famous model was the exotic Chiquita. People said she'd never been closer to South America than Southend, but whatever – in 1924 she had a little girl by him. Eve simply took the baby away and ran off with her. Augustus John got the child back, but Eve still charmed him into a vacation in Berlin, where she would introduce him to some lucrative commissions. She also made sure she got pregnant, which was why she shut the house, sacked the servants and reappeared, in 1925, with an 'adopted' baby, Amaryllis Marie-Louise. Princess Marie-Louise, a great friend, would be her godmother. No matter what it took, Eve got what she wanted.

She expected her sons to do as she wished, and Richard and Michael, the younger ones, dutifully joined the family bank. Peter, the high achiever, was easily forgiven for his decision to do otherwise because he was so talented in other directions. His success as a writer made her proud.

She saw Ian as a slacker by comparison. He knew it, and sulked. By the time he was 20, if not earlier, she embarrassed him. He knew about Augustus John, who was an old goat. He didn't put two and two together about Amaryllis. His mother had an imagination too, and her confected story about the baby's origins caused Ian no curiosity when he was 17 and preoccupied.

Eve grated on him. She was 'artistic' and wore flamboyant clothes. She had two ghastly brothers, Ian's uncles, old roués who were forever going bankrupt or getting divorced, and a whining sister.

The Roses were a wealthy family. Her father, George, a successful lawyer (the firm is now Norton Rose) was a son of Disraeli's solicitor, and her mother, Beatrice, was a daughter of Queen Victoria's private doctor. All their children were spoiled.

Eve resented her mother-in-law, Granny Kathleen, for being so stupendously wealthy. Maybe she suspected that Granny's influence lay behind her grandsons' dismissal from the direct line of inheritance – and by implication her own. Traditionally, primogeniture ruled, so once Valentine Fleming had died, custom dictated that Peter would be the heir. But old Robert was a pragmatist, and maybe he simply thought that Philip, his own second son, would make a better guardian of the family fortunes than Eve's oldest boy who obviously was not interested.

Ian liked his Fleming grandmother a lot, although she was a crazy autocrat too. Despite the forty-four bedroomed house at Nettlebed, with its vast acreage and golf course, she was parsimonious. The place was usually freezing, but then so were most English country houses. It was in her treatment of the servants that she seemed utterly dissociated from normal life by the 1930s. After the First World War, loyal staff were much harder to find. In a seller's market, the tribe of maids and gardeners and chauffeurs who supported

Granny K were paid less the longer they stayed. One account has her tipping a golf caddie with the gift of a toothbrush.

Monique, Ian's Swiss fiancée, was never invited to stay again. According to a friend of Ian's, he defiantly communicated with the girl for some time before Eve put a stop to the liaison by threatening to have his trust fund income stopped. This was a ruthless exercise of her power. He was at Reuters then, having recently returned from Moscow in triumph, aged about 24. His mother told him to break off the engagement or face living on a reporter's income. Eve had to compensate Monique's father, who sued for breach of promise, and for the sake of getting her own way, she did.

She failed a few years later in a similar action against Peter Fleming, which had enduring repercussions. It was 1935, and she had bought Grey's Court, an exquisite old house a few miles from Joyce Grove, and prepared a study in which Peter could write. Almost as soon as it was ready, he announced his intention to marry an actress. This was Celia Johnstone (St Paul's, RADA, the Comédie Française and, a decade later, an internationally known film star). Eve, petulant, self-centred and unreasonable, cut off the funds. Peter married Celia anyway.

He was not to be manipulated by blackmail. She, equally intransigent, washed her hands of Grey's Court. She sold it at once, to make sure her point hit home. In 1937 his uncle Philip Fleming decided to give Joyce Grove to Peter in any case.

• AWKWARD WITH WOMEN •

Ian's best male friend, whom he had known since early childhood, was Ivar Bryce. Bryce's background was just as privileged as his own. Bryce had the sunnier disposition and seems to have idolised his friend; he later wrote a book about him. He was occasionally shocked by Ian's patronising attitude to girls, which became more evident as time went on and Ian found conquests easier to make. Bryce recounts the distress of a glamorous young American whom Ian had picked up on his travels around Europe. He had made a flattering fuss of her, she was alone in France with him, and yet having spent several days with her and encouraged this dependency he was dismissive to the point of nastiness. He pushed her off the running board of his car and, with Bryce in the passenger seat, drove away to spend the summer in Capri.

This was typical of Ian. He was moody. He preferred the company of male friends, who were likely to be forgiving of his frequent need for solitude. Girlfriends never understood that; maybe he could not tell them. He seemed to attract girls who were needy and attention seeking. Sometimes a cat will rub its nose on your leg and twist onto its back to let its tummy be tickled – but at a certain point its claws strike deep into your hand. Ian was like that. The abuse was verbal, usually. Girls withdrew shocked, and in tears.

In a frank interview he once expressed physical disgust. In his opinion most women were not just foolish but dirty, especially English ones. He may have been right, because in freezing houses people unused to the icy morning shower of a public school certainly didn't wash enough. Conrad O'Brien Ffrench, a clever Secret Service hand who ran a valuable network of spies out of Kitzbühel, had known Ian and Peter Fleming from 1931 if not earlier, and he thought that Ian Fleming's hang-ups were beyond understandable fastidiousness. It was his opinion that, like Casanova, he despised all women once the conquest was done; by implication, he had never liked them much in the first place, for to him they were not quite human.

Was Ian becoming a confirmed bachelor? When he left Reuters and began work for Cull's, he was better off. His upstairs apartment at Ebury Street, the boundary that divided louche Pimlico from smart

Belgravia, was decorated for effect. It was intentionally dark and bookish and full of carefully placed props with which to impress visitors. There was something of the alchemist's lair about it.

He also, from time to time, borrowed a friend's flat in Marylebone Lane. There he could conduct a secret life and take nightclub hostesses or actresses to bed; he wouldn't expect to know any, socially. They were the sort of women you could ask to behave, in bed, in a way you couldn't demand of girls whose people you knew. He advised other men not to bother with actresses. They were so concerned with their careers that they were never available when you needed them.

Ivar Bryce said that Ian's girlfriends usually followed 'glamorous flirtation' with 'abject slavery' and 'fond nostalgia'. This was not the universal opinion. Some did not find the abject slavery easy to recover from and others were instantly put off by Ian's arrogance and his habit of addressing them with a sneer when they had barely met. He was very good looking, but then, so were other politer, less self-regarding men.

Nonetheless there were many girlfriends. Most were nothing more than a passing fling. Lady Anne O'Neill was one of those. She was five years younger than him and had married at 19; she and Shane O'Neill had two children. In 1936, in London, Ian got friendly with her husband and she began an affair with Esmond Harmsworth. Ian, dark and moody, she called 'glamour boy'. In 1938 they met again in Austria. Ann saw him alone in London. Neither wanted commitment.

Older women liked him better, probably because he took them seriously. Liesl and Maud were two of his older mistresses. Both were Jewish by birth, sophisticated, discreet and interested in him. They introduced him to people of influence, remained unperturbed by his fleeting affairs with other women and the very idea of a permanent union would have made them laugh. In a world where men held all the power and money, and young women had to marry a man in order to command a social life, never mind a modish hat and coat, relations between the sexes could become quite fraught. With these wise, sexually experienced older ladies, Ian felt comfortable. They were settled; they had interests beyond the bedroom; they were good company and would never make unwanted demands on his time.

In the summer of 1938 he was gainfully employed by Rowe and Pitman but enduring, at the age of 30, a kind of crisis. He had invited a girlfriend, Mary Pakenham, to stay in Capri. She hoped that the Mediterranean would put him in better spirits than usual. In London he was forever bemoaning his own perceived failure: how Peter had always been good at the things that mattered, while he, Ian, had dropped out of Sandhurst, failed to get into the Foreign Office and was now failing again and settling for a job he hated. What he really wanted was to write thrillers. The villain would perk himself up with Benzedrine, he said. The kind of thriller he liked might have a half-clad girl being whipped in it. He talked a lot about sex. He produced pornographic pictures, often featuring dominatrixes.

He was, in short, the epitome of a fixated public school boy in an arrested stage of sexual development. In the end, it wasn't his leering talk that put Mary off but his terrible manners. He had booked himself a bed in the train, while she had to sit up all night in a carriage, and the villa on Capri turned out to have no flushing lavatory. Worst of all, Ian instantly bagged, as by *droit de seigneur*, the best room.

His older women friends endured as confidantes long after they had ceased to be lovers. War seemed increasingly likely. Maud Russell, an art collector, knew that Ian was interested in secret work and would be good at it. She was herself quietly engaged in helping people get out of Germany. Conrad O'Brien Ffrench was up to something hush-hush, and so were people at Rowe and Pitman, and Sir Robert Vansittart and others that Ian saw at his several clubs. Lord Kemsley had his eye on him.

Early in 1939 it all came together.

3

THERE WILL BE WAR

· DIVERSIONS ·

In 1938, in Germany and Austria, dissidents were being removed without warning and imprisoned at unknown locations. In September, the Nazis invaded the Sudetenland. In November the world watched, appalled, as Kristallnacht shattered businesses and lives all over Germany.

In January 1939, Neville Chamberlain remained convinced that Herr Hitler was a man of his word. Hadn't he promised that we would share peace with honour? It would be a terrible mistake to put our armaments production on a war footing if no offence was intended.

Behind the scenes, certain individuals were less wooden headed, deeply frustrated by this torpor and gathering intelligence as best they could. They needed to know, among other things, whether, in the event of war, Russia would lean towards Germany, Britain and her allies or remain technically neutral but favouring one side or another. This meant getting inside Russia and finding out, and very few people could do that.

Ian Fleming was still not in the loop. He was a young stockbroker, discontented and impatient to do something of national importance, but diverting himself with his girlfriend and his book collection. The girlfriend had come back into his life; she was Anne O'Neill, vivacious, brittle, amusing, kind, brave, shallow and loud. Like Ian she had lost a parent – in her case, her mother – very young. No doubt she was invited to Ebury Street to inspect his books. Not that they were visible, for he kept the whole lot in black japanned boxes stamped with the Fleming crest in gold, but it was a remarkable treasure trove all the same, after only a few years' effort. Fleming did not spend his own time fossicking about in the overcrowded stockrooms of antiquarian dealers. He employed an expert. He had run into Percy Muir, then a quite junior bookseller, for the first time when he was about 20 in Austria. Years later when Ian had his first salary cheques from Rowe and Pitman, and

Percy had become a partner in the respected firm of Elkin Matthews, Ian asked his friend to start a collection for him. This came at just the right time; Muir was worried about the business and 'we were gradually building up a few special collections for customers who entrusted their business exclusively to us'. Fleming, whatever his faults in other respects, was loyal to people he liked.

The initial budget was £250. Muir's brief was to collect 'the milestones of progress in the nineteenth century. This set me to exploring histories of science and sociology and running to earth the original and source material for anything that had affected human outlook and habits, from the atomic theory to the zipp [*sic*] fastener, and from lawn tennis to the Mendelian hypothesis.' As John Pearson, his biographer, points out, Ian had cleverly hit on works of enormous significance that were cheap as chips:

> For four pounds they picked up one of the remaining copies of Madame Curie's historic doctoral thesis of 1903 which told the world that she had isolated radium … Other unusual rarities included Sir Humphrey Davy on fire-damp in coalmines, Pitman on shorthand, and Freud on the interpretation of dreams.

Such diversions took you only so far. Fortunately, 1939 was to be the making of Ian Fleming. His tenacity in making his ambitions plain, his obvious ability and his extraordinary network of contacts came together to put him in the position he required in order to further his ultimate aim: to write best-selling thrillers.

• PASSING THE TEST •

Fleming's former career as a journalist was well known to Lance Hugh Smith. His fascination with spying was clear to Conrad O'Brien Ffrench, painter (notably of Jamaica), Russian speaker, veteran of Mons, secret service officer and businessman. O'Brien Ffrench had been working for Claude Dansey's Z organisation, a shadowy outfit that did the work that MI6 was supposed to be doing in the immediate pre-war years. MI6 was underfunded, incompetent and badly led. Dansey had no official paid network of spies but deployed clever locals or expats like Alexander Korda to report from Europe. O'Brien Ffrench's own cover was blown when he telephoned advance warning of the Anschluss in 1938. He saved innumerable lives and got out of Austria unscathed with his family.

A trade delegation was leaving for Moscow at the end of the winter. Lance Hugh Smith, of Rowe and Pitman, told Ian that he would be leaving at that time. He was to join the press pack and write informative articles for *The Times* while ferreting out, behind the scenes, clues to the direction in which Stalin was most likely to jump; on his return to the City he would write a report, in his capacity as a concerned member of the public, to the Foreign Office.

This could lead to something; he knew it.

Russia's railways had been built on the defensive principle of an extra wide gauge. The whole delegation and press corps visited Warsaw first, then travelled to Moscow in the luxurious train normally used by Maxim Litvinov, the foreign minister. It was great fun, and Ian Fleming had a delightful time, despite having to fashion arresting news out of hours spent listening to Mikoyan, Litvinov and the British trade minister nitpicking over the price of fish. Sefton Delmer, who was there for the *Daily Express*, said he spotted the young man right away as a spook because he behaved like one. He even persuaded his new friend to come with him on a wild-goose chase to find Litvinov's flat. But beyond that – no. There were no strange meetings with sinister fellows on park benches, no discussions that began 'I see it is raining in Minsk tonight'.

Yet when, in March 1939, Fleming's report landed on the desk of the relevant Foreign Office bureaucrat, it was crisp, fact-filled and convincing. The covering note – headed 43 Bishopsgate EC2 – hit just the right note. His points were 'hastily compiled to correct the impression of some of my friends that the Russian "steam-roller" is the solution of all our problems … I am afraid you will find them very amateurish'. Well of course. No one should think he was hoping to get into the secret service off the back of this. What follows are the report's key points, omitting the figures and the caveats he cited in his text.

Emphasising that he laid no claim to solid knowledge, he pointed out that the Soviet Union's current position was defensive, not aggressive and that the Soviets needed time to grow their industrial base in order to become an effective fighting force. The population was 170 million. The USSR's strategic value to Britain could be considerable. It would lie in diverting hostile forces from the Far East, the Mediterranean and the North Sea and thereby allowing food and fuel to pass.

He reckoned the possible strength of the Soviet army was 5 to 10 million soldiers, currently under-supplied with arms of any kind. Communications along the Western Front (road, rail, radio, fuel dumps and preparation of the people and terrain) were good.

Inside the country, roads and railroads were in poor state, except on the approach to the main cities. Raw materials produced in Ukraine and the north west were accessible.

Russian air power was small by comparison with its army. A supply of better quality fuel was scheduled but maintenance was slovenly. The paratroopers were expert and there were lots of them.

The Russian navy had plenty of nimble light vessels and submarines but too few big ships; they had only one aircraft carrier so far. Large destroyers and cruisers were promised but not yet built.

Morale was low in all the services, industry and the population generally. The purges of 1937 and 1938 had upset people far more than any war.

Russians, including Stalin, would prefer Germany as an ally. Their army had been trained in Germany. They neither liked nor trusted the British. Fleming concluded that if collaboration proved unavoidable, we must sup with a long spoon.

This is a mere summary. The real thing was grippingly written and authoritative, despite the disclaimers. It proved, in the event, right about Stalin's intentions. So who were Ian's sources? If all the figures he cited had been available to a journalist who was presumably under 24-hour surveillance throughout a short stay in Moscow, surely MI6 would have had them already? It is true that MI6 was in a state of near-collapse, but even so – where did he get his information?

The figures may have been surreptitiously provided by more than one person. The foreign diplomatic corps in Moscow at the time was not allowed to leave the capital and any contact with the locals was strongly discouraged. But the Narkomindel, the Soviet Diplomatic Corps abroad, and its foreign commissar Maxim Litvinov, had found it difficult to explain away the horror of the 1937–38 purges. Key Ambassadors were recalled from all over the world – including Washington – and not replaced; others were required to return twice a year. At home, the NKVD interfered constantly. But other than Stalin, Litvinov and his diplomats must have had the closest insight into Russia's foreign policy intentions. Litvinov was old-school Bolshevik and one of Lenin's circle in his lifetime. He had lived in Britain as unofficial Soviet ambassador at the end of the First World War but had been arrested by British Military Intelligence and swapped for Robert Bruce Lockhart, the spy and journalist, in 1918. Litvinov was married to Ivy Low, who was English, and they had children already when he was deported; his family followed him to the USSR later. As an Anglophile and a Jew, he was considered suspect. Stalin's code for that identity was 'rootless cosmopolitan'.

Throughout the 1930s Litvinov had worked hard through the League of Nations to mend fences with the Allies, especially the Americans. In January 1939, he wrote a worried letter to Stalin about the damage being done to foreign relations by the lack of ambassadors, competent second-tier diplomats or even staff abroad. Stalin was unconcerned. He was preoccupied by Russia's possible co-operation with the Nazi government. He dismissed Litvinov in May of 1939 and encouraged a campaign against him and other Jews in high positions. The dismissal and the campaign were signals to Hitler that he was open to talks.

Wherever the sources of his data, this sober report on Russia's potential as an ally, or quite possibly as an enemy, was Ian's calling card. When the right people read it, doors were held wide for him. About six weeks after he submitted it, he received a mysterious invitation to dine at the Carlton Grill with Rear-Admiral Godfrey, who had recently been made director of Naval Intelligence. Another admiral, Aubrey Hugh Smith (Lance's brother) was there to introduce them.

Admiral John Godfrey, head of Naval Intelligence and Fleming's boss and mentor at NID during the Second World War. *The National Archive*

Rear-Admiral Godfrey had not yet taken up his post as DNI, but he had been busy choosing a team of over 100 people from various fields. They must above all be quick-witted and imaginative. They would be given free rein and they need have no service background. A determined, challenging approach – a willingness to think the unthinkable – mattered far more. 'Blinker' Hall, who had been head of naval intelligence during the First World War, had told him to look beyond the services for people like this, so he did.

He had been particularly struck by the way Mansfield Cumming, 'C', had relied very much on one able, quick-witted person, his personal assistant, during the First World War. Claud Serocold's tireless support had enabled Cummings to get twice as much work done. Godfrey needed somebody just like that, and he asked around, talking to – among others – Fleming's old editor at Reuters. Montagu Norman, governor of the Bank of England, of all people, confirmed that young Ian Fleming from Rowe and Pitman could do the job.

And behold, it was done. All that sly questioning of friends abroad, all the proof that he could keep secrets, all that suffering over not being good enough for the Foreign Office, all the flattery and charm expended by his mother upon the great and good – and finally, Ian Fleming turned out to be exactly who they were looking for.

· 4 ·

THE DREAM JOB

• WORKING IN A TEAM •

Ian had to be provided with a commission and a uniform. He would be in the Special Branch (intelligence and meteorology) of the Royal Naval Volunteer Reserve – the Wavy Navy, so called because of the undulating stripes that RNVR officers wore on their sleeves. The other requirements of his new employment, which would start in July, were outlined in writing by Rear-Admiral Godfrey. They amounted to gatekeeping, corresponding, knowing everybody who mattered inside and outside the service, communicating what Godfrey wanted, improving his likelihood of getting it, keeping him informed of developments, faultless record-keeping, diary management and being on call at all times. Being, in fact, the motivating engine that drove the wheel.

Fleming was outstandingly good at this. He knew everyone who mattered, or if he did not he could raid his family's combined address books. He had languages. He was ruthless – at least, in this job, ruthless enough. He communicated briskly, on one page wherever possible. He had the urbanity conferred by the City and the air of authority learned at Eton. He spotted details, recorded them, retained them and made links. He was popular, handsome, highly literate and, best of all, he liked testing fantasy solutions to knotty problems that might, or might not, arise; how to make the Germans decide you were going to invade Italy via the Balkans, for instance, or how the British Fleet in the Mediterranean would react if Franco's Spain joined up with Hitler.

By August he was officially installed in Room 39 in the Old Admiralty building overlooking Horse Guards Parade. Here, in a cloud of cigarette smoke, worked Section 17M, a top-secret department headed by Ewen Montagu, reporting to Godfrey. Their job was to interpret intercepts from Bletchley Park and messages from the operations centre across the parade ground in the Citadel. Godfrey

Ian Fleming at the Admiralty in 1940, wearing the uniform of a
Royal Navy Volunteer Reserve Lieutenant. *The National Archive*

had written 'only men with first class brains should be allowed to touch this stuff'. They were mostly journalists, artists or academics. There was no great demand for practical types or scientists; they were elsewhere, in remote locations working on biological and chemical warfare. In any case the ruling class at the time had been persuaded by their education that scientists had little imagination, rather as women could not drive a tank. It was Montagu's task to interpret the importance of the information flowing through – what the politicians absolutely must know, what could be passed on to other units for decisions about action and so on. Also, the people in Section 17M had to try to turn agents into double agents and invent imaginary agents to confuse the Germans. The fake map idea surfaced again, as a way of driving German ships into minefields around the British coast.

Ian worked alongside Ewen and had daily morning briefings with Godfrey in his office next door. 'Fleming,' said Ewen shrewdly, 'is charming to be with, but would sell his own grandmother. I like him a lot.' He liaised with the other secret services and reported what they were doing to his boss. He was the filter for 'bright ideas' that were passed on to Godfrey; if they were obviously hopeless he weeded them out. Many got through. Other wizard wheezes, some of which would prove highly successful, originated with him. 'Busy, but secretive, he seemed happy and very electrically alive', wrote Ivar Bryce, who saw him at this time.

Ian and Anne O'Neill were an item when he started work for Godfrey. (By Christmas 1939 her husband was away commanding a mechanised squadron from a base in Northern Ireland.) On the Monday night following the declaration of war, he found time to attend a dinner at her home. He was never at ease with her cynical arty friends, especially now when they took the opportunity to make fun of his uniform. He didn't respect these people, but he still minded. Perhaps because his mother's notoriety shamed him more than he ever admitted, he was sensitive to that kind of passive aggression. He was wary of 'clever' people who claimed intellectual superiority. He had a lot more respect for Admiral Godfrey and people like him. Maybe he was, as Andrew Lycett wrote, looking for a father figure: 'Since his death on the Western Front in May 1917, Val Fleming had been the ghost at Ian's feast, the blameless paragon of manly virtues whom his son could never hope to match.' Perhaps, but Ian was also loyal to the ideals that Godfrey represented.

On 8 September he was made a commander, probably in order to add authority to his briefings at high level. He knew very little about the navy, but he made friends with Captain Drake, a.k.a. Quacker, who was also in Room 39. Quacker now worked with the Joint Intelligence Committee, but he had seen action, and Ian could test his ideas against Quacker's experience.

Like Godfrey, Fleming was good at finding people who could supply particular strengths. At White's, random civilian members were dropping heavy hints about jobs in uniform. Ivar Bryce had come back from South America and asked him the same thing. 'He advised me to go back to New York and Washington, where I had some influential friends, especially in the newspaper business, ranging from Walter Lippmann to Walter Winchell. "You will be more use there," he said. "Stick around."' Bryce was perfectly happy to do that, so Fleming arranged a flight for him from Prestwick (Glasgow) to Montreal, with stopovers, and from there to New York.

Fleming wanted only people who would have special skills of value to Naval Intelligence. He was interested, for instance, in black propaganda that would deflect or deter German action. He took Sefton Delmer to meet Godfrey to talk about how to plant disinformation in the newspapers – and how to discover whether or not this ever did put the wind up the Nazis, which seemed unclear.

At the start of the war he made friends with an exceptional individual: Sidney Cotton. Handsome, in his mid-forties, Cotton was absolutely Ian's kind of man. He'd been everywhere, made money, lost it, been married, been divorced ... with Sidney Cotton, the thought was father to the deed. Like Fleming, he headed for excitement wherever he could find it. Cotton was an Australian businessman and pilot, who, in the First War, had invented draught-proof pilot suits that the RAF still wore. More recently, he had produced clear pictures of the German navy lined up in harbour and of German military airfields, having overflown these sites prepared with a cover story and piloting a civilian aircraft from which his secretary, Patricia Martin, took pictures on demand. Such photography was no easy feat, since a plane at great height is cold, and lenses mist. He had devised a practical way to keep his camera, a Leica, warm enough not to cloud up.

Ian liked Cotton a lot and was impressed. He co-opted him to do some snooping for Naval Intelligence. Ireland was a shaky neighbour. The British were dubious about the Irish Republic. It was not uncommon to hear of known German agents propping up the bar in Jury's Hotel. Fleming knew that there were deserted, sheltered harbours along the beautiful west coast between Galway and Mayo, which U-boats might find useful. It was just a hunch, but he asked Cotton to test it, photographing the entire coastline from 2,000ft. The weekend after the outbreak of war, he paid a visit to Cotton in his flat. Cotton and a co-pilot promptly took off on 12 September and took a few pictures from 10,000ft. Ian went down to Plymouth to show his boss the prints on the 14 September and was asked for the same pictures from 2,000ft. Cotton later said the following:

> It happened that A. J. Miranda had recently sold the Irish a single American anti-aircraft gun. So far as we knew, this was the only modern anti-aircraft gun they had. Miranda conducted all his European business through my office in St James's Square, so I knew all about this gun, its performance and where it was likely to be sited. My friends told me that after my flight of 12th September the Irish had mounted the gun on a railway carriage and were running it up and down the West coast in readiness for me, but I suspect they were pulling my leg.

He and his co-pilot ended up photographing the entire Atlantic coast in the next couple of weeks, and the results showed there was no need for concern.

Cotton could coolly identify a problem and find a simple solution. Uproar. The Air Ministry huffed and puffed; the RAF was responsible for reconnaissance, not the Admiralty. Cotton was dismissive. This was not the first time he had fallen out with people in authority. Quite apart from the pettiness of this squabble – after all, there was a war on – he told Fleming that the Air Ministry bigwigs should encourage the use of radar, but were blockheads who refused to be convinced. But the RAF wanted his skills on side, so he made a deal; he would be expected to go overseas at short notice, so he had to be able to get in and out of airfields easily. They gave him a special code, 'White Flight', and within three weeks of the declaration of war, he had a commission and a uniform and instructions to set up a Photographic Development Unit at Heston. Zipping over German territory in Spitfires and Mosquitos, and returning with invaluable shots of the enemy's strengths and weaknesses, his pilots became known as Cotton's Club. He told them to fly high and fast, and he had the engines souped up.

Six months into the Phoney War, the Germans had made no direct move against France or England. It was going to happen, because Germany's eastern borders were now secure because of the pact with Stalin. Sure enough, in the second week of May, Nazi units began to push back the French army. Their advance was relentless. They were soon fighting the hopelessly ill-equipped British Expeditionary Force in Belgium.

One scare had it that Germans planned to land on the beach at Southend in the weekend of 27–8 May. The Joint Intelligence Committee took this seriously. Ian and Peter Fleming (who was now PA to the Director of Military Intelligence) were unconvinced, but in case it did happen, they thought the nation deserved to get an unbiased British view of events, rather than being brainwashed by German triumphalism. So they motored down to Southend in a staff car on the Saturday afternoon, presumably with a pair of binoculars and a service revolver between them. At Southend, this being Whit weekend, they were overwhelmed by an onslaught of kiss-me-quick hats, beery East Enders and fish and chips. Having peered out to sea from a naval reconnaissance post on a hotel roof and detected nothing, they prised their driver out of the bar and returned to the comforts of home.

• RESCUER •

At the beginning of June, the Germans seemed unstoppable and the fall of France inevitable. The French navy might fall into German hands, which would be disastrous. He must have Admiral Darlan, *Amiral de la Flotte*, order it into British ports. But with the full-scale evacuation from Dunkirk in progress already, Ian was first despatched to move SIS staff out of Paris.

Among the first people he met was Biffy Dunderdale, the larger than life Head of SIS Station in Paris. Biffy had been born to wealthy merchants in Odessa. He was filthy rich, flamboyant and clever. In July of 1939 he had been one of the French and British intelligence chiefs secretly invited by three Polish cryptologists to Warsaw. There the Poles proved that they had worked out how to break the Wehrmacht Enigma code. It had been Dunderdale who conveyed this top secret information to Bletchley Park, although Fleming probably didn't know that at the time. Very few people were allowed to know that the Enigma code had been penetrated. All he probably knew was that Biffy Dunderdale, who drove his own armoured Rolls Royce, intended to evacuate key embassy staff to Jersey immediately. Ian had to deal with the rest of the SIS contingent.

As soon as he arrived, he commandeered the SIS emergency cache of money from the safe at the Rolls Royce office, and sent the staff and their families to join the growing stream of Parisians clogging the roads out of Paris. Shepherded by a Naval Intelligence officer called Smithers, the SIS contingent took refuge in a Château on the Loire.

Since Admiral Darlan and the British naval attaché were not on speaking terms, it fell to Fleming to persuade Darlan to order the French fleet to safety in English ports. On 10 June the French government fled to Tours, so he raced there hoping to see Darlan or at least an aide at Ministry of Marine. He was in contact whenever possible with Admiral Godfrey thanks to a private tele-printer line, and he told Smithers to move the SIS refugees towards Bordeaux where a British ship would pick them up.

There was no positive response in Tours. Darlan was unreachable. The government itself was about to leave for Bordeaux. Chaos reigned. Paris was in German hands by 14 June. Sidney Cotton was in Bordeaux already, moonlighting for SIS, making one of many 'special survey flights' to rescue British agents. He received urgent instructions to rescue Biffy Dunderdale and his party, presumably including the Polish cryptologists and their families, from Jersey, where they were being strafed by German planes. This would mean getting two Hudsons over there – big Lockheed bombers, which required a crew of six each, including gunners. Cotton said later:

There were reports of German planes all over the Channel, so I filled up with ten hours' fuel, flew due west at low level into the Atlantic, finally coming in via Bristol and thence to Heston. I sent my two Hudsons to pick up Bill Dunderdale and his party, then rang the Admiralty and told them of the crowds of people still stranded at Bordeaux, adding that I had seen a large number of ships at the mouth of the Gironde and suggesting that these could be used to assist the evacuation.

On the ground, Fleming was already onto it. He arrived in Bordeaux, got into the British Consulate and destroyed all paperwork that implicated French or British nationals. He then turned his attention to the refugees. He bribed a ferryboat captain, and with the help of Smithers, who'd just arrived, managed to get boatloads of people, not just SIS but also stray Jewish and other families from France, Belgium and Poland, to England. He found that seven merchant ships were moored at the mouth of the Gironde. He threatened them with being sunk by the RAF unless they helped, so they did.

Back in London, Cotton was summarily sacked. He had already clashed with Air Ministry people because of the special survey flights for SIS, and they now found an excuse to get rid of him: he'd given a lift in his RAF plane to Marcel Boussac, the head of Christian Dior. On 16 June, the day after his return from Bordeaux, he was politely informed, by letter, that Geoffrey Tuttle would be taking over as commander of the photographic unit. The Air Ministry's loss was the navy's gain, and Naval Intelligence exploited Cotton's talents for the rest of the war.

On the same day, 16 June, Darlan firmly refused British asylum for the French navy. He was already working for Pétain's puppet regime, which would ultimately move to Vichy. The French fleet was bombed in harbour at Mers El Kebir three weeks later, with the loss of 1,300 lives.

Ian Fleming's youngest brother, Michael, had been with the British expeditionary force. After Dunkirk, he was pronounced missing. In September his wife learned that he had been wounded and taken prisoner. In November, she was told that he had died at the beginning of October.

METICULOUS PLOTTING

· RUMOURS ·

One of Ian Fleming's most important tasks at Naval Intelligence was to submit ideas, however far-fetched. He would never propose a scheme by means of a detailed report that would take Godfrey an hour to read and Ian himself much longer to write. Instead, he devised his own best practice. He began by bullet pointing the general idea, neatly typed on one sheet of paper: concept, aim, results of a successful outcome, potential drawbacks. As he grew confident these missives were signed with a big bold F. If the concept were halfway to being a plan that he thought would work, he would say so and express willingness to submit more evidence and some routes for consultation, if required. Godfrey usually wanted to know more.

Fleming remained interested in rumour for undermining morale and deceiving antagonists. 'The invention of rumour is not a difficult matter. Its dissemination is', he wrote. Two outfits were already tasked with the job. They'd both been in place since before the war and neither had achieved a great deal, despite coming at the problem from a slightly different angle and working in collaboration. Department EH, at Electra House in Moorgate, was the seat of Foreign Office propaganda. The phone lines of foreign embassies were conveyed by direct cable through Electra House, and its staff, having listened in, came up with destructive rumours. Section D of the SIS, based at the St Ermin's Hotel behind St James's Park tube station, set about disseminating those rumours abroad. As far as Fleming could tell, the stories never seemed to take hold. On reflection, this is not surprising, since no sensible SIS agent working undercover in enemy territory would incur suspicion by spreading 'information' favourable to the other side.

Fleming recommended a multi-pronged approach. Any given rumour should be spread abroad by newspapers, 'Freedom' radio, diplomats and leaks to POWs in Britain, although the censors who read POWs' letters would have to be tipped off.

Effective disinformation should lead directly to desired enemy action. It was important to keep German forces occupied away from strategic targets, and Godfrey seized on one of Fleming's ideas with particular enthusiasm. In essence, it was the scapegoat ploy, thousands of years old: the goat tied to a post to attract the wolf away from the flock. But this goat wouldn't be tethered; the wolf would have to chase it. It would be a radio station broadcasting from a ship in the North Sea. 'The one infallible and inexhaustible draw for German fire', wrote Godfrey, 'would be any form of radio propaganda station.' Fleming suggested a fast cruiser, accompanied by two destroyers and air cover during limited daily hours of transmission. An alternative protection might be Q boats, the kind of camouflaged, armed, decoy boats that had had been used to deter attack in the First World War. Godfrey thought a couple of submarines would suffice, with other defences 'on call'.

They agreed that this would not be soft propaganda. There would be no attempt to ingratiate. Listeners would hear authoritative British voices speaking German, since native German speakers would give the Nazis the excuse to claim that these were German Jews telling lies. The broadcasters would explain the true situation of the German air, land and sea forces under Nazi command, and the consequences for the German people. The Nazis were always boasting about their command of the North Sea; this would make nonsense of that. 'The Germans would certainly be enraged', Godfrey noted gleefully.

So the plan had two objectives: to undermine morale in Northern Germany and to divert German troops from aggression elsewhere. Its success relied on the radio ship being able always to dodge German explosives, whether delivered by air attack or from undetected minefields.

The risk was that failure would leave the Admiralty with egg on its face and the loss of a valuable ship. (Casualties were not mentioned.) Godfrey admitted that in daylight hours, there was a serious risk of being bombed. But, he said, the service might operate only on cloudy or foggy days. He was perhaps carried away by enthusiasm.

All this was seriously considered. Questions were asked about the height and weight of masts and the best time of day to broadcast. Finally the plan was rejected as too risky, expensive and technically diffi-cult. However, the impetus for it – the perception that hearts and minds were not being converted fast enough in occupied lands – was shared by others and contrib-uted to an overhaul of black propaganda services.

• OTHER PLANS •

There were at least as many rejected plans as daring successes. In February 1940, Fleming came up with another plot. This was to flood Germany with forged currency, causing a run on the German mark, a scenario that might panic Germans into overthrowing the regime. His memo helpfully pointed out that Waterlows made the British currency and 'young Waterlow' worked at Electra House, Moorgate. This too was rejected.

Then there was the initially promising plan to steal an Enigma machine. The cryptographers of Naval Intelligence were particularly keen on this one, because although Wehrmacht Enigma (used by the German army and air force) could be read, naval Enigma could not; the German navy had been far-sighted enough to specify its own, dedicated version of the code. Ian hatched a plan to ditch a Heinkel, with a fake German crew still aboard, in the Channel within sight of a small German mine-sweeper, and once rescued, to murder the sailors and sail to Britain in possession of the boat's Enigma coding machines. He was not personally allowed to participate. Godfrey told him that he knew too much to risk being captured. However, he could direct the operation from Dover. In the event it fizzled out. Finding a small minesweeper, and the likelihood of a Heinkel plunging straight to the sea floor and taking the German-speaking crew down with it, were the points against.

He also invented plots for sabotage. In one, German ships marooned at Spanish ports were bought wholesale by British money and taken out of action. Another similar one was to buy up barges on the Danube, to prevent Germans getting access to Romanian oilfields; yet another, to scuttle other Danube barges to block Germany's access to the Black Sea and its raw materials supplied by neutral countries. After that one, German news media claimed that the Romanians had 'only narrowly' prevented British sabotage at the Iron Gate dams. It had been botched by a fellow whose grip and courage Fleming had badly misjudged.

• AMERICA NEEDS ITS OWN SPIES •

When Ian returned from Bordeaux in June 1940, Michael Fleming was missing in France and their older brother Peter seemed likely to join a shady outfit run by his friend Colin Gubbins, recently returned from Norway.

Ivar Bryce, his friend from childhood, was doing his bit, thanks to instructions from Ian to see somebody at the Passport Office on Fifth Avenue, New York. After his interview there, he had been sent to meet another Englishman at the Westbury Hotel. He was then put to work on the thirty-sixth floor of one of the Rockefeller Center buildings. His boss was William Stephenson, the British passport control officer. Bryce didn't at first know the significance of that title; he claimed later, perhaps disingenuously, that he thought he was working for 'an obscure branch of the Consular Service' on their Latin American desk. He did notice that all continents were dealt with and different staff were forever coming and going.

Late in 1940, Bryce was told that he was to work in South America recruiting agents for a new operation, the Special Operations Executive. After Dunkirk, Section D, Department EH, and another outfit devoted to guerrilla warfare and sabotage, had been combined into the much better resourced SOE. It worked out of the old Metropole Hotel on the corner of the Strand and Northumberland Avenue and ran both male and female British and foreign agents who were engaged to live as civilians abroad while gathering information and assisting, where necessary, in guerrilla warfare, propaganda, resistance and sabotage.

Across the Atlantic, the international department in the Rockefeller Center was known in London as BSC, British Security Co-ordination. William Stephenson, code name Intrepid, had been in post for a long time, and despite tireless diplomacy, the Americans still were not in the war. Ewen Montagu's wife, Iris, the daughter of Victorian artist Solomon J. Solomon, had worked for Stephenson in New York before war began; even then they had been busy turning out black propaganda aimed at Nazi sympathisers in America and other propaganda aimed at getting USA to join in. But still, for preoccupied Americans in Idaho or California, Hitler was a long way away.

Stephenson, himself a Canadian, knew Hitler really was not. He was worried that this vast, rich country, still smugly convinced of its own exceptionalism and invincibility, lacked a full-time spying service of its own. Roosevelt agreed.

For the first fourteen months of the war, the US Ambassador in London was Joe Kennedy. Kennedy had been a convinced appeaser in the 1930s, and now he insisted to all Washington – especially after Dunkirk – that the British were definitely heading for defeat. American resources must be reserved for use at home.

Roosevelt nevertheless decided that the US must look after its interests in the rest of the world or

America would be stuck between two expansion-
ist powers: Japan on one side and Germany on the
other. He asked General William J. Donovan to set
up a secret service along the lines of the British one
– really secret, its mere existence unacknowledged.
General Donovan was a former Wall Street lawyer,
popular and clever, a man of wide interests and pleasant temper. He travelled to London in 1940, and
many times after that, to find out as much as he could
from the Joint Intelligence committee meetings and
the security directors involved. When he returned, he
confirmed to Roosevelt that Kennedy was wrong. The
British were a bulwark against oppression and they
needed money. Roosevelt lent it to them, in exchange
for 99-year leases on base stations worldwide.

Joe Kennedy and his family fled London for the
country when the Blitz began in September 1940. This
made him extremely unpopular in London, where
even the King and Queen and their children stuck it
out, and by November he was no longer ambassador.
Kennedy's views continued to find favour in America,
though, and he was dead against an international intelligence service.

• GOLDENEYE … GIBRALTAR, 1941 •

In August 1940, after his visits to France and America, Fleming began to plan Operation Goldeneye. A couple of months before, Spain had stopped being 'neutral' in favour of the suspicious 'non-belligerent'. Madrid, Lisbon and Gibraltar were pullulating with spies and counter-spies. The British urgently needed reliable watchers in Spain. If Franco were to join the Germans, Naval Intelligence must be fully prepared with a secret unit in Gibraltar to commit acts of sabotage and communicate with friends on the mainland. If the Germans ever gained a foothold in Andalucia, across the narrow Straits from the positions they already held in North Africa, they would undoubtedly mine, and otherwise block, the passage to the Mediterranean. For this reason Gibraltar was among the most strategically vulnerable locations of the war.

Ian visited Madrid in February 1941. His contact there was Alan Hillgarth, naval attaché, another of the many adventurers who at this time ended up in the British diplomatic service. Hillgarth was a good friend of Winston Churchill, and an accomplished spymaster. He knew everybody, ran agents and greased palms generously and to good effect. He had successfully incentivised contacts in key positions, including Spanish generals and senior government officials.

Hillgarth discussed the Spanish political position with Fleming. Sam Hoare, the Ambassador, a pre-war appeaser, was terrified of offending the pro-Nazi side in Spain. The Government was pretty well evenly divided in its loyalties. Franco himself owed Germany a favour since Hitler's government had supported him in the Civil War, but he was a pragmatist.

Fleming initiated a cypher office in Gibraltar, to link it with London. Gibraltarian civilians were being evacuated, fortifications reinforced and the Rock, with its tunnels, occupied by some of the 30,000 service personnel to be stationed in Gibraltar. The place presented a formidable defensive position. History recorded that succeeding occupiers had held it for hundreds of years at a time. But Fleming wanted to know how far the German navy had already arranged to hinder shipping in the Straits. And recognising that a successful invasion of the Rock by Axis units could never be ruled out, he also installed a back-up unit in Tangier.

In Spain he met William J. Donovan for the first time. The American general was on a 'fact-finding tour'. If Donovan were to make a successful pitch for a big, expensive new secret intelligence department, he would need to have its architecture drawn up by someone with a good understanding of what such an entity could and should do and how to do it; and Stephenson had recommended Fleming. Fleming was keen. He also suggested they should work as an Anglo-American Joint Intelligence committee to co-ordinate efforts to invade North Africa – when possible; at this time the US had no official foreign intelligence service and was not on a war footing.

In May of 1941 Admiral Godfrey flew to America with his assistant, Commander Ian Fleming. Fleming and Godfrey arrived at La Guardia at the same time as Schiaparelli, and quite by accident they ended up in the background of her picture in *The New York Times*, taken by a paparazzo. They had rooms at the St Regis, then owned by Viscount Astor, who was in a position to talk about intelligence to Roosevelt. They were to see Stephenson at the Rockefeller Center, and discuss with him, and American naval officers, the security of American ports.

Ian 'introduced Godfrey to the Morgan banking clan', as Andrew Lycett succinctly puts it. Together they went to the fashionable 21 Club. They read the news that HMS *Hood* had been sunk by the destroyer *Bismarck*. A couple of days later, the *Bismarck* was sunk. New York suddenly seemed rather unreal.

Fleming had discussed Donovan's plans and needed time to write his blueprint; Godfrey wanted to confront Hoover of the FBI in Washington. Smithers was already there and by-passing the naval attaché, whose assistant he was, to gather secret intelligence about the Japanese and send it back to London.

Ian later told Ivar Bryce that when he got to Washington he was 'locked in a room with pen and paper'. He produced a précis and a full seventy-page document:

> ... a detailed blueprint of the British service, using a century's experience of its aims, its methods and its security. It was a tour de force of organising and administrative ability, and demonstrated what I believe was Ian's greatest strength ... For clearly expressed, practical, administrative talent, with no detail omitted, and no conceivable eventuality forgotten, he had no equal.

Godfrey saw that Americans liked Fleming, so he left him behind in Washington with a brief to do a lot of socialising and produce 'clear and practical' memoirs for Donovan. He told Ian to emphasise the all-round vision required of the ideal intelligence officer, and the need to get your staff lined up before you opened shop. And of course he had to keep his collaboration with Donovan quiet. If Donovan should be seen as a British stooge, Roosevelt would never get the idea past Congress

Roosevelt gave Donovan some seed money, and Donovan gave Fleming a .38 Colt service revolver inscribed 'for special services'. But Pearl Harbor had yet to happen and the Office for Strategic Services would not officially exist – or Donovan serve as its head – for another year.

Bryce, meanwhile, was still in South America under orders from Stephenson. Stephenson feared that the Germans could too easily invade Brazil from Senegal, across the South Atlantic. He was unconvinced that any South American government was fervently committed to freedom and democracy. Several Latin countries harboured Nazi cells. Mail to and from Europe was generally offloaded in the Caribbean and censored by the British (Conrad O'Brien Ffrench was in charge in Trinidad) before being sent on. The one regular, un-monitored channel of communication was a weekly plane from Dakar, Senegal, to Recife, Brazil, where it refuelled for the return journey. Stephenson wanted this service put out of action, which was easy enough if there was no fuel in Recife. Bryce tricked a friendly old caretaker at the airfield into allowing him to slip through to the fuel store, where he planted a bomb and left. The entire supply went up in a sheet of flame.

Bryce also 'doodled' a map of what a Nazi South America would look like. Both he and his boss saw its potential as propaganda. They happened to know that Germans in Cuba maintained radio contact with U-boats in the Caribbean. They even knew where the German base was. They passed on that information to the FBI, but not before they'd planted a map there, forged by experts, very like the one Bryce had made. It added to the drip-feed of propaganda but still failed to undermine Middle America's opposition to war.

In June 1941 the Soviet Union came in on the Allied side. Ian wanted to be sent to Moscow, but the leader of the British military mission there wouldn't have him at any price. In his view, Fleming was gullible, a nuisance, and spoiled.

There is one odd postscript to Fleming's blueprint for the OSS. In July 1975 *The Times* claimed in its obituary of Dick Ellis (later suspected of having been a double agent) that Ellis had been decorated by the Americans for the OSS blueprint.

Whoever wrote it, the contents must have boosted Donovan's campaign to start a secret service. He faced angry political opposition, because anything that smacked of a secret state sounded like Communism to Republicans, and Hoover, in charge of the FBI, was deeply suspicious on principle of anything the British liked. William Stephenson was well aware of this, but he urged Donovan to persist. The British needed America on side, but they didn't need an ally that leaked like a sieve.

• PROPAGANDA AND OTHER PREOCCUPATIONS •

When Fleming returned to England, he turned his attention to the Political Warfare Executive, the PWE. This was set up to feed 'white propaganda' to the BBC German Service and to transmit black propaganda through its own radio station, GS1, Gustav Siegfried Eins, to encourage rumours to spread among the German population and U-boat crews in particular. Material from Naval Intelligence's interrogators inspired much of its output. Ian's friend Sefton Delmer, formerly of the *Express*, had been working for it since the start of the war. His parents were Australian, but his first language was German, and GS1 was presented by an imaginary Nazi. It was highly successful, although the convincing 'Fake Nazi' caused a collective raising of eyebrows in Whitehall. Ian's own broadcasting career was short-lived and not wildly successful, since in December of 1941 he recorded a confident talk for the BBC German Service and the following day, HMS *Repulse* and HMS *Prince of Wales* were sunk off Malaya. Godfrey had commanded the *Repulse* for three years until 1939.

The winter of 1941–42 was relatively quiet. The Blitz was over and the V-1s and V-2s had not yet begun. At Christmas there was something to celebrate. Pearl Harbor had kicked the USA into action at last. In the spring, there were Americans in uniform everywhere, officers in the Berkeley Bar and ratings strolling through Piccadilly and Leicester Square.

Ian had moved to a tiny flat in Athenaeum Court, overlooking Green Park. He was seeing Anne O'Neill and several other upper class young women, as well as Maud Russell. Muriel Wright, for whom he'd found a Whitehall job, had been a model before the war. He found her rather dim, but he had persuaded her to take his 17-year-old sister Amaryllis riding regularly in Richmond Park.

Anne was resident mostly at the Dorchester, where Ian often played bridge with her and her lifelong friend Loelia Duchess of Westminster. The Duchess, who was separated from the Duke, had a crush on Ian that does not seem to have been reciprocated. She was six years older than him and had been a 'bright young thing' in the 1920s. He never could take her seriously as a seductive older woman, but he did immortalise her as the matronly Loelia Ponsonby in the Bond books. It was Maud Russell for whom he had real respect and affection, and it seems to have been mutual. She gave him a keepsake that he treasured: a gold cigarette case, disguised by a coating of gun-metal. She understood his love of deceit.

• THE OSS AND JAMAICA •

Rear-Admiral Godfrey was to be kicked upstairs at the end of September 1942; promoted to vice-admiral and sent to Bombay, his job at the Admiralty placed in safer hands. Like Cotton, he was a man who did his job outstandingly well but whose abrasive self-confidence caused offence. Ewen Montagu, who liked him, said he was 'a shit, but a genius'. Before leaving his post, he found it necessary to go on Naval Intelligence business to New York, and he took Ian Fleming with him. They visited the thirty-sixth floor of the RCA building in Rockefeller Center, and at William Stephenson's apartment they met Ernest Cuneo, the lawyer and former footballer who would become Ian's lifelong friend. Ian was to be Naval Intelligence's liaison officer with the OSS in London, and in New

York, Junius Morgan, of the banking family, was his opposite number.

Godfrey flew on to Canada, and Ian made his way to Washington. In October there was to be an Anglo-American joint conference in Jamaica. Ian had never visited the island, although both Conrad O'Brien Ffrench and his mother's lover, Augustus John, had been inspired to paint it, and he may well, before the war, have seen some of those paintings. And in the 1930s, Ivar Bryce had bought Bellevue, a mid-eighteenth-century plantation house, in Jamaica. He would be attending the conference too.

Bryce had just arrived, and was at the airfield to meet Fleming off the plane from Washington. With the coming of war, Bellevue had been largely unoccupied except for one live-in caretaker-housekeeper. Rather than leave him to sleep at the Myrtle Bank Hotel in Kingston with the others, he took him back there. It was a 10-mile drive away, in darkness over bad roads and in a tropical rainstorm. Bellevue, as the name indicates, was on a hilltop. When they arrived they had to park the car down the hill and haul their own suitcases up to the house before getting in, shaking themselves dry like dogs and awakening the housekeeper to provide some refreshment. It was hot and rainy 'to the point that little toadstools appeared in our leather shoes during the night'. Bryce felt dreadful. He wished he hadn't suggested this.

That first night, they sat on the veranda drinking grenadine and water and waiting for the chicken to be cooked. They stared out at a deep starry sky through curtains of rain splashing relentlessly off the roof. Behind them was a tall gallery, 65ft wide by 65ft deep, with 'a double door and two windows penetrating the bookshelves and giving access to the hurricane room' behind. Admiral Lord Nelson had convalesced there after a fever.

In the morning, the sky had cleared. They could look down the hill across miles of tropical flowers and trees to the port of Kingston and sunshine sparkling on the blue Caribbean.

They ate chicken and drank gin just about every night, and bought a lot of fruit. Ian seemed happy. He and Bryce left for Washington in the same plane. Bryce wrote:

Having gone over and over his notes with intense concentration for hours, he suddenly snapped his brief-box shut and turned to me sparkling with enthusiasm. He paused. 'You know, Ivar, I have made a great decision.' I waited, nervous of the news to come. 'When we have won this blasted war, I am going to live in Jamaica. Just live in Jamaica and lap it up, and swim in the sea and write books. That is what I want to do.'

He asked Bryce to find him 10 acres or so, away from towns and on the coast. Bryce promised to get his agent, Reggie Acquart, to look for somewhere. Then he forgot about it.

· 6 ·

MORE WAR

In London, Ian worked long hours. Anne O'Neill had been living in the country with her two children while her husband remained in Northern Ireland. She had seen less of Ian since the beginning of the war. She was still having an affair with Esmond Harmsworth, the second Viscount Rothermere, a divorcé with three children who was fifteen years older than she was. At the start of 1941 she had given a New Year party at the Dorchester, where she sometimes stayed; Ian was among the guests. Ian was lucky in the Blitz, although he had narrow escapes from raids at the Carlton, at Sefton Delmer's flat in Lincoln's Inn and in Dover. His flat at Ebury Street, with its skylight high on the roof, was not properly blacked out, so throughout the winter he stayed at clubs or hotels. One night, after a dinner and frightened by bombs falling in the West End, Anne decided to spend a night at the Lansdowne Club with him.

It was not a *ménage à trois* exactly; there was no *ménage*, but in the spring of 1941 there were *vacances à trois*, since according to Anne, she and Esmond and Ian took an unfortunate holiday in Cornwall together because Ian bullied them into it. They drove, and she was carsick all the way, and miserable. Perhaps Ian wanted to re-live the happy summers on West Country beaches that he had spent with his brothers, of whom only two were left.

• INVASION FROM NORTH AFRICA •

When the Blitz had largely stopped and the Americans came into the war at the end of 1942, Ian watched as the most fascinating ruse of all took shape. When Ian first joined Naval Intelligence, he had written a long list of ideas for deception and sabotage, mostly original. Many of these had been considered and shelved or put into effect already, but one at least had seemed, perhaps, too bizarre to tackle on any occasion. On his list, Ian had credited it to a plot in a Basil Thomson novel of the 1920s, in which a dead body is left to be found, so that the information it is carrying will send the finders on a wild goose chase.

The plot was again put forward in the summer of 1942, this time by one Cholmondeley, from Montagu's team. Nothing much happened. But circumstances would make Naval Intelligence look again.

Donovan's new OSS was in place and still viewed with suspicion at home but in constant contact with British intelligence. Roosevelt wanted the attack on Germany to start in Europe, right now. The British were adamantly against this. If they could seize North Africa from Casablanca to Cairo, they would be able to invade Italy and fight northwards through the occupied lands of southern Europe, including France, before attacking closer to the Fatherland itself. Roosevelt saw the point and conceded it.

So in September 1942, the Allies were united in determination that Operation Torch, the invasion of North Africa, should go ahead as soon as possible. A date was set, and in September, a courier set off by plane from England to Gibraltar with secret documents: most importantly, a letter from General Clark, in charge of the Allied Expeditionary Force, to the island's governor that told him to expect Eisenhower on the 'target date', 4 November. The plane crashed. A few days later the courier's body was washed up on a beach in Southern Spain. The letter from General Clark was still in his pocket, unopened.

Had the Germans, in fact, opened it? Would they have been forewarned of the attack?

Technical experts decided not, and observation revealed no giveaway build-up of German patrols. Holding their nerve, the British ordered Operation Torch to go ahead. It worked exactly as planned.

The courier was dead, but the macabre Thomson/ Fleming/Cholmondeley idea – of the body with the false clue – had come to life again. It was used in Operation Mincemeat. The Germans needed to be tricked, and fast, because as soon as North Africa was fully under control, the dimmest German school-boy with a map would spot the Allies' next move – on Sicily, which offered the easiest of landings conveniently opposite the shores of Libya. Just such an invasion was planned for the summer of 1943.

Could the Germans be duped into defending a different invasion point, or even two? Probably, but a plot would require scrupulous attention to detail. A body was obtained, that of a poor derelict Welshman who had died alone in King's Cross. Sir Bernard Spilsbury, the pathologist, advised on making it credible as a drowned man, and on the conditions necessary to mislead Spanish or German pathologists as to cause of death. A name was chosen – a common enough name that did, in fact, belong to more than one officer in the services. The corpse was to be a major. The uniform and boots fitted, the underwear – obtained from someone who'd been hit by a tram – was well worn. A backstory, supported by correspondence, identity tags and documents and random indications of the deceased's origins and character, was concocted, and a fake Most Secret letter.

Ewen Montagu and others in Room 39 involved were having rather a good time, carefully putting together a convincing persona to be stuffed into the dead man's pockets. The penultimate touch, a love letter with a fiancée's photograph and a bill from Phillips in Bond Street for the engagement ring – along with scolding letters from father and bank manager – came close to over-egging the pudding.

The Most Secret communication was the one the Germans must seize upon. It would outline a projected pincer movement of invading forces from the Balkans in the east to the South of France in the west. There was some concern about concealing this sealed personal letter (genuinely written by the Vice-Chief of the Imperial General Staff) because the entire effort would be wasted if, as in the genuine incident last September, the Spaniards didn't open it. The consensus in Room 39 was that the Operation Torch courier's mail had remained undisturbed because Spanish people were Catholics and unwilling to disrespect the dead. The plotters decided that their particular major would therefore carry the valuable letter separately, not in his pockets. He would keep it with other valuable documents in a briefcase secured by a chain loop of the kind that normally runs across the body and down the sleeve; bank messengers in the City used something similar. But who would wear such an uncomfortable thing on a plane journey? Instead the leather-wrapped chain was carelessly, but tightly, tied to the belt of his greatcoat.

Luck was on their side. A couple of British planes did crash at about the right place, at about the right time, before the body was found, complete with associated briefcase. And thanks to a little nudging from Hillgarth's network of influential locals, the body, and the letter, found its way to German strategists, who were convinced. The Allies knew they would be expected in Sicily, so they were going to land in the South of France or in the Balkans – the Germans had proof of it. They deployed their defensive forces accordingly. So when British and American servicemen landed in Sicily in the summer of 1943, they were able to move relentlessly on through Italy with little opposition.

Fleming had the satisfaction of having devised Mincemeat in the first place, but he was busy, by then, with something more important.

• COMMANDER FLEMING'S COMMANDOS •

Before Operation Torch and the invasion of Africa, and Operation Mincemeat and the successful advance through Sicily, there had been a test run. In the summer of 1942 with the Office for Strategic Services officially instituted, Roosevelt insisted on an immediate invasion of Northern Europe by British and American forces. Churchill was adamant that this would not work; it was too soon. But he could not prove it. The idea of invading Europe from Britain, right now, had to be tested before Roosevelt would be convinced.

A crack commando unit would therefore carry out a small, targeted raid on a German post in north-west France. Its stated aim would be to capture intelligence – cypher codes, handbooks, equipment worth investigating – and leave. Its unstated aim was to test German defences.

The crack commandos would be men of outstanding ability and initiative: 30 Assault Unit (30AU), the brainchild of Ian Fleming. He would watch from a destroyer offshore and report on the outcome. This worked perfectly. He wrote the battle description as it happened, and the commandos, with heavy losses, made it back to Newhaven. This proved that invasion by the even the most competent force, 30AU, might fail. Nazi defences across the Channel were currently too strong to be tackled. They must be reduced, and diverted elsewhere, before an invasion along the Channel coast. Roosevelt gave in.

30 Assault Unit probably had its roots in Peter Fleming's experiences of the Independent Companies – territorials who had worked to great effect in Norway in 1940 and 1941, laying mines to entrap U-boats – and the Auxiliary Units, undercover groups from the Home Guard he had set up with Colin Gubbins. Ian's 30AU, made up of three troops of marines, sailors and soldiers respectively, included exceptional individuals.

Education and experience had made Ian a passionate elitist. He had come across a lot of clever people like Cotton by 1942, enough to hand pick such men and make a crack commando unit out of them. They would usually be deployed in an intelligence capacity, that is, capturing materiel and data that could be used by cryptologists and saboteurs. Every man was strong and athletic, intelligent and resourceful, and ideally fluent to native-speaker standard in a second or third language. Many had unconventional backgrounds. They were trained in parachuting, safe-cracking, lock-picking, searching of persons and care of prisoners, and facial recognition techniques. They learned how to behave should they be captured and how to react under interrogation. The Navy troop, while being trained 'on general Commando lines' took courses in enemy sea mines and torpedoes, electronics and the essential layout of submarines, among other things. They all learned Italian (daily lessons before Sicily), and individual skills such as photography were known and exploited.

30AU as a whole were to find and retrieve certain items from locations targeted on a Black List; these were required for, to quote Fleming, 'hastening the decisive defeat of Germany and Japan the improvement of Allied naval equipment ensuring that Germany and Japan shall not be in a position to fight a third war'.

Each fast-moving section of 30AU should know what to look for. They would capture wireless receivers, plans, technical handbooks, operators' logs, instruction books, radar equipment, cypher books and machines, and in particular, anything to do with new weaponry. They would demand these things from living Germans and riffle through the clothing and possessions of dead ones. At the invasion of Sicily, having claimed its hoard each troop collected it in one place and shipped it out.

As war ground on through 1943 and 1944, 30AU was supposed to infiltrate occupied territory, and even Germany, in order to discover more about the atom bomb that the Germans were working on.

They were also tasked with sabotage operations. Records exist of a plan to sink seven enemy ships out of the eight that lay at anchor in Las Palmas, Canary Islands. Eight trained Polish men would sail into the harbour on a ship that was under British control. The skipper of the Danish ship *Slesvig* would be paid to wait for 'passengers' (the Poles) who were expected to arrive soon. Under cover of darkness, the Poles would dive into the harbour and place two limpet mines on the hull of every ship, including the British one, except for the Slesvig. These mines had a three-hour time delay. The Polish saboteurs would not hang about. They would climb aboard the Slesvig and sneak away.

Meanwhile the crew of the British ship would take to the lifeboats, and as soon as their ship went down, they would row ashore and report to the British Consul as Displaced British Servicemen. They were to deny any knowledge of other personnel having been aboard.

The raid on France by 30AU was the nearest Fleming ever really came to seeing action. The Las Palmas plan would have killed a lot of people. The question that arises now nags: did Fleming fully understand the key fact about destroying an enemy as rapacious as Hitler – that if necessary, you must be prepared to match him in cruelty? Was Fleming personally the sort of person who would do that?

He delighted in violence in the privacy of the bedroom. He liked to bully masochistic women mentally, as well as physically. And, as he later proved, he could imagine torture and murder. He had that internal shard of ice that enabled him, as a writer, to withdraw and observe most situations. He lived through the Blitz without panicking. Yet there is no evidence that his job ever took him into the London Cage in Kensington Palace Gardens, where British officers tortured German prisoners to extract information, or to the suburban houses of the Combined Services Interrogation Centre. As to killing someone, his invention, James Bond ('licensed to kill'), would admit of himself that he 'never liked doing it'.

Somebody certainly passed POWs to him for interrogation of a gentler kind. There were people in Military Intelligence (Guy Liddell was one) who were pretty sure torture was less effective than the velvet glove. Ian was good at soft-soaping people. Wearing civilian clothes, he would take captured German U-boat commanders, who presumably were elegantly shod and given suits from decent tailors, to lunch in smart restaurants. In theory, rare beef and several bottles of Romanée-Conti could work wonders and probably did, until one day, when he and two such guests were enjoying an animated conversation at Scott's in Mount Street, they were interrupted by Scotland Yard detectives. A waiter, hearing conviviality in German, had called the police, and Fleming and his friends were hauled away in a Black Maria. He never entirely lived that down in Room 39.

JAMAICA

· What to do Next ·

Captain Edmund Rushbrooke, Godfrey's successor in the autumn of 1942, seems to have encouraged Fleming to carry on much as before, as Commander of 30AU – in command but never in the fight.

His job in wartime is often described as 'desk-bound'. This is very much an elastic term. Throughout his naval service he had continued to draw a salary from Rowe and Pitman, and he kept in touch with City contacts. So that was some long lunches sorted; then there were the cocktails and dinners with his OSS liaison officer in London, Lieutenant Tully Schneider, at the American Officers' Club in Park Lane. He was seeing a pretty colleague called Joan Bright at the time. At 38, and doing rather well on his own, he saw no point in marriage. Women, he told Schneider, were 'like dogs; men were the only human beings, the only ones he could be friends with'. He did admit to being badly upset when Muriel Wright was killed by a bomb.

He visited Cairo, a hub of British intrigue in the Middle East, for the Churchill-Roosevelt conference in November of 1943 and Joan Bright went along. A month later he and Anne were both Christmas guests at Send, a quiet, dispersed old village near Guildford, where Loelia Westminster lived at Send Grove.

In 1944, Anne would receive news of Baron O'Neill's death in action. Eve Fleming had lost her husband when she was 38 and had lived on a generous allowance ever since. Anne O'Neill was 41 when she was widowed, and there wasn't a lot of money. She was miles from being poor, but in order to maintain her lifestyle and social position she needed a rich husband. The two favourites, had London society been opening a book on it, would have been Esmond or Ian. People were hard pressed to say which, but they probably thought both men were terribly well off. Esmond was extremely rich, but he and Anne were forever bickering. Ian was reluctant to marry and anyway hadn't inherited the income Anne would require. His grandfather had left him and his brothers out of his will and his grandmother died intestate.

Ian did not make a move. That winter he was travelling with Clare Blanshard, Hillgarth's assistant, in
the Far East. But as the Allies began to bomb Japan
the Nazi threat to Britain diminished. The end of the
war in Europe was within sight and he was thinking
more and more about how to live when it was over.
His job was being slowly wound down. In 1945, the
mundane tasks were all that remained. Typical was a
day he spent in Malvern, reporting on the office and
accommodation proposed as home for staff of the
Royal Signals and Radar Establishment. He delivered
a caustic but constructive two-page assessment of the
state of HMS *Duke*, which had until then been a Royal
Navy shore base. To sum up, the lavatories were dis-
gusting and all its scant facilities required an upgrade.

He tied up the loose ends of his naval career and
considered the future. He would carry on training
with the RNVR. The Cold War began soon after the
hot one finished, and nobody was completely sure, for
a long time, that hostilities would not break out somewhere. Godfrey still lived at No. 36 Curzon Street and
gave dinners to which he invited members of Naval
Intelligence – men only, of course. There they could
reminisce and talk shop for as long as they liked.

Just as Ian was beginning to relax, Anne received
a proposal. In 1945 she told him she would marry

Esmond Rothermere. They would live at her house in Montagu Square.

Ian took a flat in Montagu Place. Anne, as Lady Rothermere, was financially secure, and returned to doing what she did best — entertaining what the French would call a salon of artists and writers, mostly witty, not particularly intellectual but good, if slightly bitchy, company for her and for one another. She invited Peter Quennell and Lucien Freud, Duff and Diana Cooper, Evelyn Waugh and Noël Coward, Stephen Spender, Barbara Skelton, Felix Topolski, Cyril Connolly and many others. She was far from happy with her husband, but she understood Ian and knew that, like a cat, he was attracted to women who didn't seem to want him. Ian was just around the corner, and since he did not appear to enjoy himself much with her crowd, he was not always invited.

• REFUGE •

Ivar got in touch, quite suddenly. Reggie Acquart thought he'd found the perfect property. Could Ian come out and see it?

Ian could. Reggie, a Jamaican by birth, took him to see what Bryce called 'a fourteen-acre strop' — a long narrow piece — on the island's north coast about a quarter of a mile east of the village and harbour of Oracabessa. This was a village, a 'free village' founded by the famous abolitionist James Philippo in the 1830s. Nothing much ever happened there, except when banana boats called in from time to time. The locals had a jolly time then, loading green bananas onto the boats, getting paid and partying long into the night. 'Oracabessa was fast asleep between these calls.'

There was a shack on a clifftop near the village end of the 14 acres. A garden's length in front of it, and 40ft below, was the ocean – with a white sand beach and an underwater reef with tropical fish flashing in and out, just visible through clear water. Ian was enchanted. On a rock sticking up from the seabed grew a few wild plants: a single fragrant Portlandia, with its dancing bell-like blooms, and the local weed, Shamelady (so called because if you touch it, it shrinks away). The beach was inaccessible except by boat, but anyone who bought the land could have steps cut in the cliff.

Ian agreed the price by cable. The strip of coastline with the shack on it would cost £2,000 sterling. The future he'd imagined for himself on the plane back from the Kingston conference, in the middle of the war, had never left his thoughts. In Jamaica, in his own house, alone, he would find peace and quiet and write spy stories that would make him rich and famous.

Now all he needed was an income of some sort, and something rather better than the shack to live in.

The war had allowed him to outgrow his childhood. The RNVR was family now. The Flemings of course were still part of his life. Amaryllis, the little sister in whom he had not shown much interest until she was a teenager, had proved to be far more of a rebel than her brothers. She resented Eve, the woman she had been told was her adoptive mother. Nobody knew, said Eve, who her father was. Eve had her own half-baked reasons for telling these lies, but as a result of them Amaryllis felt lonely, rejected and defiant.

At Downe House School, which she loathed, she had spent every spare moment playing the cello and lived for her regular trips to private lessons at the Royal College of Music. She had performed on BBC radio when she was 15 and completed her education at the RCM while performing as a soloist. When the war ended she was 20, and managing her own career. It helped that she was a beautiful redhead of outstanding talent, but she still struggled to find work at first and asked both Eve and Peter for an allowance to see her through. Both refused, saying she should join an orchestra to earn her keep, but she knew she would be trapped if she did that.

She was determined to be recognised as a unique talent while she was still young, and she went on to become one of Europe's leading solo performers, partly by investing in herself. She paid for tuition from others of great merit. One of those was Pierre Fournier, with whom she had an affair. He was married with a child and the same age as Peter Fleming. She later said that the Fournier tuition had come to abrupt close when Peter discovered their love affair and visited the cellist in his London hotel room. There was a lively exchange of views, after which the white-faced lover called the whole thing off, telling Amaryllis that he would never feel safe as long as he feared that one of her brothers might come after him with a pistol. What she did not know, but Peter almost certainly did, was that during the war Fournier had earned generous fees by performing on a German-funded radio station that broadcast to Vichy France.

In 1945 Peter and Celia Fleming were living in Oxfordshire and bringing up their son, Nicholas, aged 6; they would soon have two daughters as well. Celia had reservations about Ian. In 1940, when Peter was an officer in the British Expeditionary Force in Norway, the *Daily Sketch* had reported his death in action. Eve and Celia were devastated, and Celia

never got over a suspicion that Ian could have prevented Lord Kemsley from printing such an error.

Peter remained a popular author. At the start of the
war he had found time to write *The Flying Visit*, a gentle
satire in which Hitler floats down from the sky somewhere in the Home Counties. After much puffing and
sliding and scavenging across muddy countryside he
arrives at a village hall where a talent contest in full
swing. When he takes the stage everyone thinks he is a
comic turn and he wins a pound of butter. Much put
out by being laughed at – and dismissed as a disgrace
by his pre-war admirer Lord Scunner – he is captured
and kept as a prisoner of war. Upon his deportation
the German government, having employed a double
in his absence, sends the real Hitler back.

Peter Fleming's war opened in the Grenadier
Guards and ended in India and the Far East. In
between, among other things, he was engaged by
Lieutenant-Colonel Gubbins to help set up the
Auxiliary Units, secret commando-type units of
the Home Guard that would become active only in
case of invasion. Members of the Auxiliaries were
trained in sabotage and guerrilla warfare. They were
the military predecessor of 30AU, and many of the
soldiers had served in The Independent Companies
in Norway.

Richard went back to the bank. It seemed that you did not need to be a financial genius to run a merchant bank after the war. If you were family, you took advice, and you sat on the Board, and you made decisions based on that advice. There were no major mergers or acquisitions, no upheaval. The City went on much as it always had, with the clearing banks doing what they did, and the Barings, Rothschilds and Flemings occupying their own niches.

Eve had become eccentric. At the start of the war she had chosen to live in an old abbey in Berkshire that was supposed to be haunted. Her companions were her crotchety maid Hilda (the one who called her 'The Great I Am') and, in the school holidays, sulking Amaryllis. The house in Cheyne Walk was shut up, and later on it was hit by a bomb, so in 1944, when the German attacks had died down, Eve took a flat in Knightsbridge. The following year she moved to No. 21 Charles Street, a smart Mayfair Georgian terrace with four storeys and a basement. She was in her element again, overseeing its redecoration. And Ian moved quite soon to Hay's Mews, which was not only close to his mother's house but to Godfrey's convivial dinners in Curzon Street too. Amaryllis was a frequent visitor to Hay's Mews, and according to Fergus Fleming, she met plenty of girlfriends coming and going. 'They ran his baths; they fetched his lighter off the mantelpiece; and they cooked salmon kedgeree, which he sent them to learn from his mother.'

• THE INCOME •

At the end of the war Ian was offered a suitable job with a high salary: working for Lord Kemsley as head of foreign news for all thirty or so papers in the Kemsley group, including *The Sunday Times*, which was then based in Grays Inn Road. He took it, on condition that he might spend two months of every year in Jamaica. Kemsley agreed. Ian would be a manager, information gatherer and occasional contributor. He brought glamour and connections to the post.

In Fleet Street at the Rothermere group's *Daily Mail*, Anne was directing Esmond, according to *Time* magazine. Esmond had managed to quell the pre-war appeasement stance of that paper – these days it supported Churchill – but his new wife was often called 'imperious'. She acted like a newspaper magnate *manquée* but had no idea of financial or other considerations. 'Annie's boys', who included Peter Quennell, were, on the whole, good journalists. They got an extremely generous salary and expenses.

Ian commuted by car from Hay's Mews to *The Sunday Times* offices. Weekly editorial conferences were held at the start of the journalistic week on Tuesdays. They were chaired by Lord Kemsley, who besides being the owner was also editor in chief. Ian's job meant appointing foreign correspondents and making sure that their articles were syndicated to papers all over Britain. All his reporters would have a few pieces on the back burner, and he would be in touch with key players before the weekly meeting to get a precis of breaking news in capitals across the world. He would have a rough outline, always subject to change, of the following Sunday's foreign coverage, and Kemsley and the other editors would indicate approval or otherwise.

On the wall of his office at Grays Inn Road there was a map of the world with all eighty correspondents pinpointed by flashing lights. The whole room had a military, battle command centre look to it. Some of the Kemsley journalists would have felt quite at home, because they were still being paid by MI6. Ian wanted gripping reports written with economy and vim. He didn't want fluff. His reporters must be likeable, good companions who were genuinely interested in all sorts of things. He would have no alcoholics, no blabbermouths and no invalids.

And yet he was low on self-discipline. There were certain rules that he could never apply to himself. At 38 he was already subject to chest pains. He reportedly drank a bottle of gin every day and smoked seventy cigarettes. This was 1946; research that linked cigarettes to cancer was largely ignored even by doctors, and the link between smoking and heart disease would not emerge for a couple of decades. At Hay's Mews he had what were called 'kidney problems' and possible 'heart weakness'. Doctors were consulted, but nothing much seems to have been done about either condition.

• THE GILT WEARS OFF •

Most of his enthusiasms lost their appeal to Ian in the end. The affair with Anne remained exciting because they could arrange clandestine meetings in exotic places. (She had been with him in New York in 1946 when he complained of chest pains.) They could visit Ivar and Jo in Vermont or stay together in Paris, where she'd got her brother a job on the *Daily Mail*. There was passionate correspondence about his sadism and how much she loved his beatings.

At work, he was nobody's darling. After a few years other staff began to mutter that his foreign news reports were tired – just copies of wire stories. Ian did not put himself out to be one of the boys; chumminess had worked well for him in 1933 in Moscow, but now his focus was elsewhere. He was not to be found with Scotch eggs and a pint at the Yorkshire Grey but preferred lunch at his club. He sometimes wore, caddishly, a polka-dot bow tie. He felt somewhat detached from *The Sunday Times*. He thought Kemsley was allowing standards of journalism to slip. He preferred to involve himself with *The Book Collector*, an academic journal that Kemsley had bought, as a distraction.

Most of all, he was glad of the annual chance to get away.

• TWO MONTHS OF THE YEAR •

Ian had his mother's confidence in her own taste but his Scots grandparents' asceticism (in matters other than tobacco and spirits). Old Robert and Granny Kathleen, and their sons including Val, had been forever striding miles across moors in the teeth of a gale. According to Andrew Lycett, 'when one Englishman dined with them in Scotland, he likened the experience to eating alongside muscle-bound bolts of tweed'. Ian wasn't a great walker – he liked cars too much for that – but there was certainly something of the hair shirt in his attitude to comfort. For alongside the Flemings' hardiness ran parsimony. Granny Kathleen did not simply inhabit a series of under-heated houses. She did not allow guests' sheets to be washed between their visits, but had them left on the bed. There were three taps on the baths: hot, cold and – for economy – rainwater. As to her husband, who gave Val a quarter of a million on his marriage, he spent – in the same year – just £6,500 on wages for the 150 staff at their various homes.

So when Ian designed a house for the plot in Jamaica, which he did – without an architect – he designed his own Brutalist vision exactly as he wanted it, with no nonsense about hot water. Or, indeed, glass in the windows. Or carpets. Or a fridge. Or even floor paint; the concrete floors were blackened with boot polish that came off on the soles of your feet. Somebody suggested he call the place Rum Cove.

Others liked 'Shamelady'. He called it, of course, Goldeneye. He had constructed something that sounds rather like a concrete blockhouse, which since he had recently spent five years staring across Horse Guards Parade at the Citadel is not surprising. Goldeneye had a sloping roof above one big reception room, several small bedrooms, cold showers and a small kitchen. It was all on one level. Instead of glass there were slatted blinds – jalousies, which rattled in the wind. It must have been a beastly shock to stay in, especially if you were Loelia Duchess of Westminster and didn't like huge flying insects. Chilly nights, which do happen in Jamaica, the wind and the rain off the ocean, must have made the indoors bleak, and as for the outside elevation, Noël Coward – who lived further along the coast – declared that it looked like a National Health Clinic. He called it Golden Eye, Nose and Throat.

It is pretty enough now. Chris Blackwell, who has known it all his life, has it. But in the 1940s locals watched with relief as vegetation rambled all over and covered it.

Reggie found him a live-in cook-housekeeper, Violet, a comfortable woman. Ian would get up early and swim. After an excellent breakfast of paw paw, Blue Mountain coffee, scrambled eggs, and bacon, he would read. At around midday, he swam and snorkelled and looked for lobsters for lunch. Ackee and saltfish, curried goat and grilled snapper were Violet's repertoire, and he liked them all.

Among the first visitors, in 1947, were his mother and his half-sister Amaryllis. Eve was fascinated by Jamaica, since Augustus John had been inspired by it before the war. Amaryllis gave a recital with piano accompaniment by Miss Foster Davis, whom they invited to lunch afterwards at the Myrtle Bank Hotel. All the other guests in the room got up and left when the Flemings and Miss Davis were shown to a table. They were white, and Miss Foster Davis was not. Eve, furious, whispered to her 'take no notice'. Amaryllis recounted this shameful incident and said later that it was one of the few times she'd been proud of her mother.

They were unprepared for the rigours of Goldeneye, with its forbidding aspect and the legs of the beds standing in jars of water to keep ants out; they weren't crazy about Violet's curried goat, either. They fled to the Montego Bay Hotel and ran into Noël Coward, who sympathised.

Ian was 40ish, with some health issues, but still smoking sixty or seventy cigarettes a day. He had done so for twenty years at least. He would carry on smoking at the same rate. So to imagine him eating or reading or even swimming is to remember that he punctuated his every activity by lighting, smoking, waving around and stubbing out cigarettes. There was always a pack by his side.

He was the least considerate of hosts. He would set off in the mornings with Anne in a boat and not return until the evening. Loelia, playing gooseberry back in the blockhouse, had nothing to do except read, and despite her vast financial resources lacked the will to find anything. In the end she too packed and left for a hotel.

Ian had other visitors. Jamaica – with Coward living there, and Lord Beaverbrook, William Stephenson and Tommy Leiter, who had become friends with Ian in Washington – was increasingly attracting wealthy individuals. Ivar Bryce had married the fabulously wealthy Jo Hartford. Her brother owned Paradise Island in the Bahamas. She had an exquisite old house in Nassau as well as a place in New York State on the border with Vermont. In 1949 they decided to take a Caribbean cruise with some friends. On the way they would call in at Goldeneye, where Ian was in residence with a girlfriend.

Their party disembarked in Oracabessa Harbour. The friends were taken to a hotel while Jo and Ivar left for Goldeneye. Later that night, returning from dinner along the coast in Ocho Rios, they passed the captain on shore amid an agitated crowd – the entire population of Oracabessa – and their yacht, wrecked, in the harbour.

The sorry story was told. Unknown to the passengers, in the first days of the trip down the east coast, it became evident to the captain and engineer that the yacht company had hired a bunch of clowns to crew with them and they were the only people who knew how to run the ship. All the way here, they'd had to take entire responsibility for the yacht's safe journey. Ocorabessa had been the one night when they knew the visitors wouldn't be coming back. Both captain and engineer took their chance to go ashore. The crew, in a ship moored in a calm harbour, would look after it. What could possibly go wrong? It had occurred to neither of them that the crew might raid the bar, drink it dry and smash the boat up.

This was the night, over a nightcap later when the women were in bed, when Fleming told Ivar that he was planning to write his first book. He'd been thinking about it since he was a schoolboy. It would be a spy story and the hero would be a British secret agent.

Anne usually went to Jamaica when Ian did but they would leave and arrive separately. In 1949, her departure had been noticed in the newspapers. When she got off the boat from New York at Southampton on her way back, a man served her with a 'cease and desist' notice from Esmond. She was married to Lord Rothermere and had to stop seeing Ian Fleming. 'But,' she protested to her friends, 'he knows Ian Fleming has been my lover for fourteen years.'

· 8 ·

SHOTGUN

• TWO BIG STEPS •

In the first month of 1952, Ian told Amaryllis that as soon as Anne's divorce came through, he would marry her. Amaryllis was appalled. She disliked Anne, and they both knew it. He told her there was no alternative. Anne was pregnant. She and Esmond had been separated since October, so the child was his. He didn't tell her that in 1948 Anne had had a baby which didn't live, which had been his too. Esmond Rothermere knew, even then, but not until the 'cease and desist' notice did he take any action.

Ian was enough of a Fleming to consider the future from every financial angle. He had always wanted, and with a child on the way actively needed, to make a lot of money. He had once said that his ideal woman would

The 'real James Bond', the American ornithologist whose book *Field Guide to Birds of the West Indies* gave Fleming the name for his own 'Master-spy'. *Philadelphia Enquirer*

be about 30, kind, Jewish and with an independent income. A younger version of Maud and Liesl, in fact.

Anne was 38 and came encumbered by extravagant tastes plus two school-age children by Shane O'Neill. She looked what people call 'hard-faced', and the tight little hairstyles, vivid lipstick and rigidly tailored clothing of that era didn't help. 'She really is very handsome and well-bred, but no sex appeal,' observed Barbara Skelton.

But they were to marry March 1952, and he would have to write the book. Now. He thought about how to do it and worked out, as he always did, a plan. The idea of writing a spy novel had apparently been in Fleming's mind for a decade before he finally decided to commit the book to paper. Little did he know the phenomenon he was about to create when he sat down behind his typewriter on the morning of 15 January 1952 to start the first chapter of *Casino Royale*. Working alone at 'Goldeneye' there would be no distractions. He knew the plot and the characters; he had been thinking about them for years, deliberately noting aspects of people he had met, especially during the war. He would type 2,000 words five days a week for six to eight weeks. He would work in the mornings and under no circumstances stop to look anything up. In the evening he'd make corrections. On the shelf in his study was the book that had gifted him the name of his hero, *Field Guide to Birds of the West Indies*, by the ornithologist James Bond.

Fleming told Leonard Mosley, a contemporary at *The Sunday Times*, that he had created James Bond as the result of reading about the exploits of the British secret agent Sidney Reilly in the archives of the British Intelligence Service during the war. He had apparently learnt a great deal about the operational history of NID from the departmental archive, including its role in the greatest intelligence coup of World War One – the cracking of the German diplomatic code 0070, which possibly gave him the inspiration for Bond's

Sidney Reilly, from the 1931 *Evening Standard* serial 'Masterspy'.
Evening Standard

own code number 007. His interest in and knowledge of NID case files from World War One enabled him to draw on a rich seam of characters, experiences and situations that would prove invaluable in creating the fictional world of James Bond.

One of Fleming's wartime contacts, for example, had been Charles Fraser-Smith, a seemingly obscure official at the Ministry of Supply. In reality, Fraser-Smith provided the intelligence services with a range of fascinating and ingenious gadgets such as compasses hidden inside golf balls and shoelaces that concealed saw blades. He was the inspiration for Fleming's Major Boothroyd, better known as 'Q' in the Bond novels and films.

Having a fascination for gadgets, deception and intrigue, Fleming had always been particularly attracted to the 'black propaganda' work undertaken by the Political Warfare Executive, headed by former diplomat and journalist Robert Bruce Lockhart, with whom he also struck up an acquaintance. In 1918 Lockhart had worked with Sidney Reilly in Russia, where they became embroiled in a plot to overthrow Lenin's fledgling government. Within five years of his disappearance in Soviet Russia in 1925, the press had turned Reilly into a household name, dubbing him a 'Master Spy' and crediting him with a string of fantastic espionage exploits.

Fleming had therefore long been aware of Reilly's mythical reputation and no doubt listened in awe to the recollections of a man who had not only known Reilly personally but was actually with him during the turmoil and aftermath of the Russian Revolution. Lockhart had himself played a key role in creating the Reilly myth in 1931 by helping Reilly's wife Pepita publish a book purporting to recount her husband's adventures. As a Beaverbrook journalist at the time, Lockhart also had a hand in the deal that led to the serialisation of Reilly's 'Master Spy' adventures in the *London Evening Standard*.

He stuck to the plan. The first draft must be written fast. As he wrote in Jamaica he absolutely must not allow himself to be sidelined into research or concerned by detail.

He stuck to a formula. He had read dozens of books of the kind he wanted to write. He instinctively knew the general structure of a thriller, the need for a dramatic dilemma, big action scenes, reversals of fortune and suspense before a triumphant outcome. He knew the essential characters. As a schoolboy he'd read John Buchan and 'Sapper' and William le Queux, and knew he needed a patriotic protagonist who was a braver, better-looking, more accomplished version of the reader, and a

James Bond as he first appeared in the first *Daily Express* strip cartoon serialisation of *Casino Royale* in 1958. *Daily Express*

The second incarnation of James Bond used in the Daily Express strip cartoon serialisations from 1960–62. *Daily Express*

lethal antagonist about whom everything was alien. But all that *Boy's Own* stuff was from the 1920s. He'd got to add plenty of sex to make it work for the fifties – like Harold Robbins with *Never Love a Stranger*. There must be women, impossibly seductive and if possible bound and gagged as on the lurid covers of *True Detective*. And – because the British audience were living in a grey world – a strong dose of material aspiration. The British were riveted by enormous wealth. *Daily Express* readers were fixated on Lord and Lady Docker because of Bernard Docker's enormous yacht and astonishing Daimler with hydraulically operated hood, and his wife's mink and diamonds, former husbands and seamy past as a showgirl. The same people read the William Hickey column because it was about aristocrats who turned up at race meetings and parties. Cars, hotels, beaches, women: James Bond must consume them all, conspicuously.

He wrote *Casino Royale* 'to take my mind off other matters'. He completed the 62,000 word manuscript in a little over two months, and when he thought it was readable, he took it back to London and married Anne, who that summer received a £100,000 settlement from her ex-husband.

• GETTING PUBLISHED •

In May 1952, he had lunch with William Plomer, a friend who worked at Jonathan Cape. He told him about the book but said it wasn't quite ready. Maybe, that first time, it wasn't. But after a short enticing period during which the manuscript was always not quite ready he eventually delivered it. The reaction was favourable. Cape would take it, with small revisions.

He proved to be the kind of author that publishers dread. He behaved – even to the august Jonathan Cape himself – rather as if he had paid Cape and they were hired labourers. Maybe he genuinely thought that he was doing them a favour; a lot of first-time authors do, although they live to be disabused of the illusion.

First of all, he did not accept their qualified acceptance. He accepted their revisions, but the book needed other changes, he said, before they could have it. He did the editing, wrote a whole new chapter, and re-delivered. They were satisfied. He then insisted on designing his own cover. It turned out to be cleverly deceptive. It was a charming image – sea blue, with parallel trails of crimson hearts down either side, and a central crimson heart enclosed by a wreath with the words 'whisper of love'. Only the title indicated that this would be other than a soppy romance.

He was forever on the phone, finding out what was going on with his book and suggesting ideas for marketing it. In the most charming way possible, of course – but while the editor is talking to an author, an editor cannot be getting on with anybody's book.

He had none of the authorial embarrassment about money that was so unhealthily inspired during the Romantic period and endures to this day. He was not distracted by vanity. He had written *Casino Royale* for fun and money, and the cheques would not be forthcoming unless the marketing and sales were right. He kept his thumb on Jonathan Cape's neck. With Ian, the more profit he made, the more careful he got. Without an agent, he took advice from a solicitor, and became, with Anne, joint director of Glidrose, the company that held copyright and to which all film and television rights would be assigned.

In the long term, Ian Fleming really was doing Cape a favour, and the huge success of his early books owed a lot to his own drive in talking the book up and exploiting his networks – making sure that before the book appeared in 1953, review copies would go to all the right people. Raymond Chandler complimented 'the best thriller writer since Eric Ambler. Ian Fleming has discovered the secret of the narrative art ... the reader has to go on reading.'

Fleming was on the phone again, demanding a bigger print run.

Ivar Bryce noticed that it was well reviewed, and extremely popular: there were three printings because of rising demand. Even so, he though it 'gave little notice to the publishing world of the torrential rain of gold gathering strength over the horizon'.

Fleming asked Bryce to find an American publisher for him – one willing to put in the effort and shift a lot of copies. 'I am not being vain about this book, but simply trying to squeeze the last dirty cent out of it.' Doubleday took the bait. Ian may have asked Paul Gallico, too, because he put in a word. Gallico, the massively prolific storyteller, loved the book anyway; he had already referred Ian to his own Hollywood agent. Things were going pretty well. 'My signature is beginning to look more and more like Shakespeare's' Ian wrote. He could be quite funny when things were going well.

Cape offered him a three-book deal, but he didn't bite. He thought he could get a better offer elsewhere. Because he didn't think they were pushy enough, he insisted on contributing to their advertising budget for the book. He added a third as much as they'd been willing to spend. But Cape were British. America was a vastly bigger market, and in his view, the Britishness of Bond was his unique selling point; he was nothing like the usual gumshoe of American detective fiction. And since the USA had only recently got its own dedicated spy service, it had no spy-fiction genre. There had never been an American Scarlet Pimpernel, Richard Hannay or Bulldog Drummond. The things Bond knew and the way he behaved would be a revelation, he thought. There was also the class advantage: hadn't Ivar Bryce, old Etonian, managed to attract one of the wealthiest women in America? Americans in the forties may have thought a cut-glass English accent meant 'a faggot', but American women found it sexy. In Ian's experience they did, anyway. They would love the laconic, precise manner of Bond's speech in the book.

Macmillan published *Casino Royale* in New York, after minor editorial tweaks, in 1953. It sold, though it didn't set the world on fire. Elsa Maxwell, whom the Flemings knew, gave it a good review.

In London he continued to seek distraction from his job at *The Sunday Times*. He got involved as a publisher with the Queen Anne Press, which produced the work of many friends – Patrick Leigh Fermor, Diana Cooper, Evelyn Waugh, Barbara Skelton and Cyril Connolly.

Eve must have been rather proud by the end of 1952. First of all she had a new grandson, Caspar. Ian had named his son after the Admiral Caspar John, the

only boy born in wedlock out of Augustus John's four-
teen-odd offspring. Peter, who wrote for *The Spectator*
these days, had published *A Forgotten Journey*, Ian had
had *Casino Royale* accepted and Amaryllis Fleming
was the toast of the town. She had spent her career
so far touring with ensembles and trios and quar-
tets, constantly learning and winning prizes. She had
been taught by some of the great cellists of her time,
including Pablo Casals and Pierre Fournier.

In 1952, she won another of many prizes, and Eve
hired the Wigmore Hall for Amaryllis Fleming's début
as a star. The hall was packed. All her half-brothers
were there, and so was Princess Marie-Louise.
Afterwards there was a big party at Fortnum and
Mason. Amaryllis was launched. That summer she
appeared at a Promenade concert with the Hallé at
the Royal Albert Hall, and bookings came in from all
over Europe. They continued to do so for decades.

A few years after that night at the Wigmore Hall,
she confronted Eve about her parentage. Eve denied
it. In the end it was Augustus John who, after much
hesitation, admitted that she was his daughter. She met
and spent time with the rest of the John half-siblings,
including Caspar and his sister Poppet John. Poppet
was one of the Connolly-Skelton-Freud-Topolski set,
who were friends of Anne Fleming.

Amaryllis would go on to become one of the world's leading cellists. It is often said that her career did not fade until the arrival of Jacqueline du Pré.

· 9 ·

TECHNIQUE

· GLAMOUR ·

When his second book, *Live and Let Die*, was published to much applause in England in 1953, Ian exulted. The James Bond series could run and run. 'It is the freshness of the situations I put him into that are most important'. It was also the glamour. Writing the book in Jamaica the year before, he had handled a particular talisman every day. It was a gold-plated Imperial type-writer, a unique object he'd ordered as a present to himself after *Casino Royale*.

It stood on his desk as a reminder. The British craved luxury. Their clothes had not come 'off ration' until 1949, and confectionery and sugar were still rationed. Consumer goods from abroad – silk stock-ings, imported records, new drinks and cameras and cars – were a revelation. Anything from America or even France seemed better designed, glossier, silkier and vastly more desirable than the grey flannel, peach underwear and brown paper that Britain was still wrapped up in. Britain was cold, with grey light. The Clean Air Act had not been passed, and London was foggy six months of the year, the buildings soot-blackened, the rain-spattered windows brown, skylights still blocked with blackout paint. Single, bare electric light bulbs cast shadows in living rooms. Ugly British Standard paint colours were ubiquitous. A fresh 'look' was slow to arrive. Crowds at the Festival of Britain saw how clever designers could exploit tiny resources. Paper quality had declined during the war, and British illustrators had become expert at making arresting wallpaper and book illustration that could be printed in only three or four colours.

People craved light, laughter and better food. From October to May, vegetables stocked by a high street greengrocer would be turnips, swedes, parsnips, cabbages, beetroots, sprouts, onions, carrots and potatoes. There would be no garlic, or anything at all out of season; if you wanted peas, they came in a tin. Only the smartest restaurants imported food and good wine from abroad. Cars were still usually black. Luxuries were out of reach to almost everybody.

Austerity could not continue, and the British were eager for change.

So the gold-plated typewriter, and his gunmetal cigarette case which was really gold as well, reminded Ian of the glee his readers felt when James Bond ordered a vodka and tonic, noticed Revlon bottles in a lover's bathroom or roared away in a speedboat. Revlon isn't an upmarket brand today, but it was an exotic American import then. You couldn't get vodka in the pub either. Most people had never tasted it.

• INSIDE INFORMATION •

When Bond saw a character with 'brand new Ben Hogan clubs' his readers already knew enough about the golfer who owned them to guess that those must be the best set you could buy. Knowing the significance of a brand implied experience of other options. You knew the best, because (in your exciting life) you'd tried the rest. If you didn't keep up with what James Bond knew, you were a hick, because if the business you'd founded with your demob money went well enough, you might get invited to join a golf club, and thanks to Ian Fleming you would know what clubs to buy. James Bond would always be one step ahead. He knew so much that he had his cigarettes specially blended, which was awe-inspiring. If James Bond had a camera, it would be described with precision; perhaps Minolta Minox, a tiny apparatus that few people would have heard of before and even fewer could afford.

Fleming hit on the difference between new money and old. New has to be told the right label to buy. Old has had years of experience and hunts down the item that satisfies his unmet need – in Bond's case, for miniaturisation and a good lens.

In Britain, in the fifties, people wanted to know about glamorous things because they were looking forward to a better life. As well as social sophistication, James Bond offered a kind of street-wise canniness. He passed on a few tips about criminals. From James Bond, you found out how card sharps cheated ('he wore no signet-ring for pricking the cards, no surgical tape wrapped round a finger for marking them'). Ian gave readers vague hints about tradecraft – false names, codes, that sort of thing. With insider nuggets like that to hand, you could impress your friends even if you'd never played poker or deceived a soul in your life. In this confusing post-war world there would be no flies on you. You'd be suspected of having a hidden hinterland, thanks to Bond. Also, Bond was unshockable. 'A pleasant-spoken Import and Export agent called Blackwell had a sister in England who was a heroin addict.' Goodness. Imagine making such an observation so casually. You didn't know anyone, even at one remove, who was a heroin addict.

• IMAGES •

Another writer might put, for instance, a fat man alone in a bar. Fleming, through Bond's observations, can build a whole background from the sight of that fat man before he has shifted his buttocks on the barstool. Like Sherlock Holmes, Bond makes deductions because he can; he knows so much. Through his eyes we notice that the fat man's nails are perfectly manicured; that his skin is white, like someone who never leaves the casino or the underground lair; he is short, so Bond thinks he might have a Napoleonic superiority complex; His suit is stretched across the shoulders, implying 'repressed power'; and so on. Every picture tells a story. Whether or not these judgements are rational or correct, we don't care; we've suspended our own judgement in favour of James Bond's.

Young women in Fleming's books don't wear many clothes but when they do, it's black lace rather than utility knickers and a set of hair curlers. A girl may be literally killed by gold, and of course she is an excuse to display diamonds. There is not much detail here; the reader – usually a man – can supply his own fantasy, but the wrapping is yet another expression of riches and luxury. A female character may be put firmly in her place at the commencement. 'Be a good girl and …' It was how Fleming often addressed the women in his own life. They seemed to like it.

He avoided giving readers any clues about real-life trickery that had worked. Ewen Montagu would undoubtedly have put his Operation Mincemeat on the desks of the right people before he published it in 1954, but Ian avoided sensitive material in his fiction. As to the extravagant gadgets, Ian once said that because he had worked in Naval Intelligence, he knew exactly how far he could go. In the real intelligence world, bag drops in parks did take place, and surveillance, and clandestine meetings with agents as well. His art lay in giving nothing away: getting them slightly wrong, either too obvious or too outrageous to be believable in real life. The same applied to gadgetry. Swordsticks could be bought in London shops, miniature cameras really were used, rooms were bugged and commandos did carry knives in their socks.

MI R(C) had been instituted during the war especially to come up with weapons for 'irregular warfare'

— it was known as 'Churchill's Toyshop' — and the OSS set up a special department for working on this kind of thing. Ian simply took an idea and put knobs on it.

• SNOBBERY •

M makes a dismissive show of not being able to understand 'our currency and bullion reserves and all that'. Gentlemen didn't: it was vulgar to discuss money. At least, so the reader is supposed to assume, though in fact Ian Fleming knew better than to open the traps: either boring the reader or revealing big holes in the plot. James Bond (Eton and Fettes), confronted with the prospect of a lecture on how all this financial stuff works, 'felt boredom gathering at the corners of the room'. Fleming himself had been a lazy student. If your family owned a bank, there really wasn't much reason to understand how it worked; people were employed to do that sort of thing. Years later, at Ian's memorial service, Amaryllis had organised everything and the choirmaster required payment — 10 per cent of £100. Richard, then chairman of Fleming's, wondered aloud how much that was.

This was no doubt mere affectation, but it wasn't entirely a joke. Not understanding money was loaded with meaning. It signified that filthy lucre was so easily come by, you didn't need to bother about it. Another version of this underlay the inverted snobbery of the writers Anne knew, some of whom were not ashamed to live in comparative squalor, because it signified that they were artists, and an artist's inspiration was somehow sublime. Ian made a fetish of being mercenary over the books because he wanted to make it quite clear to Anne's sneering friends that he had no literary pretensions. In later years, he once walked in on a bunch of them when they were giggling over a particularly purple passage of his – making it sound a lot sillier than it was. He was humiliated. He couldn't win. They could pretend to great art while living in a hovel but had no compulsion about drinking his wine in his smart four-storied stucco terrace near Buckingham Palace while feeling free to despise his work.

And then there was science. He was deeply interested in the outcomes achieved by practical people. He had not personally been educated in that way; he was no Sidney Cotton. In Fleming's social world, people on the whole showed no enthusiasm or much curiosity about science, or engineering for that matter. So James Bond drove some pretty swanky cars but probably couldn't have described the workings of an internal combustion engine. He was ten years younger, roughly, than Ian Fleming but had Fleming's generation's outlook. At

Eton, when Fleming was there, Science was all one subject, until you were about 17, when you could also do
biology. And even if you intended to become a doctor,
you couldn't get into medical school without Latin. It
seemed more gentlemanly to specialise in the humani-
ties. This outlook persisted, despite decades of protest
that the German Gymnasia taught science much better,
and certainly well enough to give German industry a
massive advantage before the First World War.

• IN-JOKES •

In *Casino Royale* Le Chiffre ('the total amount'), the
villain, was allegedly inspired by Aleister Crowley, the
humourless old drug-addict, self-styled wizard and
alleged murderer, rumours of whose bizarre rituals
thrilled London society in the 1920s. Eve may well
have invited him to her parties in Chelsea, for he was
quite a pet of London sophisticates at one time. Ian
had known him during the war.

Each of Fleming's characters was generally inspired
by more than one real person. There are several con-
tenders for James Bond himself, for instance. But the
in-jokes were in the names. In all the books he ever
wrote, he used the names of characters from his own life.
A John Blackwell, a friend of his, was related to the

Patrick Dalzel-Job, one of several influences that contributed to Bond's fictional personality. *The National Archive*

woman who became his lover, and the real Blackwell was unlikely to have had a heroin-addicted sister. A Mr and Mrs Bryce appear as a couple on a train. Ernest Cuneo, the lawyer, is a cabbie called Ernie Cureo. Smithers, who shepherded the SIS families across France in 1940, becomes Colonel Smithers, head of research for the Bank of England. James Bond himself, an American ornithologist, lunched at Goldeneye with his wife early in 1964. And poor Tom Blofeld, member of Boodle's and chairman of the Country Gentleman's Association, had his name used for an evil genius intent on taking over the world.

Architect Erno Goldfinger, whose name Fleming commandeered for the villain of his 1959 novel. *Washington Post*

Fleming came a cropper with Goldfinger. Erno Goldfinger, the modernist architect, was not noted for his sense of humour or equanimity of temper. He perceived, in the character given his name, sniping anti-Semitism. He engaged lawyers. They wrote a letter. Fleming retorted that in that case he'd call the character Goldprick and include a note to say why, which was unnecessarily rude. But it all died down, and Goldfinger withdrew, with his costs paid by Fleming, before the case came to court.

• PLOTS •

Fleming's plots – sub-plots were largely absent – had to involve life or death struggle. Both James Bond and his terrifying antagonist must have everything to play for and sometimes in the course of a real game. Baccarat, bridge and golf featured, and were games that Ian knew well. The big picture was the one that Fleming, who had conjured intrigue throughout a world war, was always aware of. So both parties, whether SMERSH or Goldfinger or British Intelligence, had to have access to shatteringly powerful means of destruction. Fleming knew he was an ignoramus about all this, and he had to stay the right side of science fiction. Whatever he came up with must be able, potentially, to work. So a shark really would have eaten a man, a limpet mine did exist and would blow up a ship, and a single individual who knew what they were doing (such as Bond) really could re-direct a nuclear missile away from a target. Everything must be checked and sources consulted. This was not easily done from a remote village in Jamaica, so the plots were carefully mapped out and researched as far as possible in the months before writing began. His recollections of reading First World War NID case files and his first-hand Second World War experiences seem too to have provided a wealth of ideas and plot inspiration. Documents that came to light in 2008 involving British spy chief William Melville's 1914 investigation of a possible German plot to blow up the Bank of England's gold reserves to bring about economic chaos in Britain may well have sparked a thought in Fleming's mind that led to his Fort Knox *Goldfinger* plot. Indeed, Gustav Steinhauer, Melville's German opposite number and author of the Bank of England plot, bore all the hallmarks of Auric Goldfinger's Teutonic persona. Known as 'M', Meville was another character, in addition to Admiral Godfrey, who may well have influenced Fleming's thinking in terms of Bond's fictional boss.

Fleming was, without doubt, heavily influenced by real life events that were mostly within the public domain, but occasionally events that were, at the time, beyond the knowledge of the general public. He started in his first book *Casino Royale* as he meant to go on. There were a string of incidents in the book that were all based on fact. For example, the attempt to assassinate James Bond outside the Hotel Splendide had its root in an incident a decade before. SMERSH, the Russian espionage agency he had initially chosen as 007's nemesis, had given two Bulgarian assassins box-camera cases to hang over their shoulders. One was red leather and the other blue. SMERSH had told the Bulgarians that the red case contained a powerful high-explosive bomb and the blue one an equally powerful smoke bomb that would allow them both to escape under the cover of the ensuing smoke screen.

One assassin was to throw the red bomb and the other was then to press the button on the blue case. However, the Bulgars decided to play safe and press the button on the blue case first, thus concealing themselves in the smoke screen before throwing the bomb. In fact the blue case also contained a powerful explosive device and both assassins were blown to pieces. This concoction was not as far-fetched as it sounded.

In fact this was very similar to the method used in a Russian NKVD attempt to kill the German ambassador to Turkey, the former Chancellor Franz Von Papen in Ankara on 24 February 1942. On that occasion the assassins were also Bulgarians and they too were blown to pieces while Von Papen escaped with only superficial bruises. Other real life events that influenced Fleming plot lines were the tunnel from West to East Berlin that enabled MI6 to tap the Russian telephone system, the KGB spy Khokhlov and his bullet firing cigarette case and the MI6 diver Buster Crabb, who dived under the Soviet cruiser *Ordzhonikidze* in 1956.

On the other hand, he had no qualms in telling readers that certain events or locations referred to in the books were true or the background to a story accurate when he knew full well they weren't. In *From Russia with Love*, for example, he dramatically began his narrative with an 'Author's Note' to the reader in which he claimed that SMERSH was a top secret department that actually existed at the time of writing and was a massive Soviet counter-intelligence organisation employing some 40,000 agents in Russia and abroad. He further claimed that SMERSH headquarters was, in that year of 1956, located at No. 13 Stretenka Ulitsa in Moscow and that his description of the building's interior that was to be found in Chapter 4 was 'faithfully described'. Nothing, however, could have been further from the truth. SMERSH (a contraction of Smert Shpionnam, meaning 'death to spies') had in reality only existed for three short years between 1943–46 as a small sub-section of the NKVD. No. 13 Stretenka Ulitsa was an address he had chosen at random and was actually a tsarist-era public apartment building that remained as such until its demolition in 2003. Likewise, the man who Fleming reveals to be its real-life chief, General Nikolai Grubozaboyschikov, was a non-existent figment of his fertile imagination.

He was, however, the first to admit to an honest error. While the proof readers and editors at publishers Jonathan Cape did their best, a certain amount of technical errors managed to evade their eagle eye. Readers in particular, loved to write in to him pointing out, for example, that Vent Vert is made by Balmain and not by Dior, that the Orient Express had vacuum and not hydraulic brakes and that you have mousseline sauce and not bearnaise with asparagus. Such mistakes, he told the *Daily Express*, were really nobody's fault except the author's and caused him some degree of embarrassment to see them in print. He consoled himself, however, in the belief that the majority of the public either didn't mind the occasional error or more likely, didn't even notice them.

When it came to delivering a plot line, a little like Agatha Christie, Fleming experimented with the method of telling a story. In the *Spy Who Loved Me*, written in 1961, for example, he made a dramatic departure and told the story in the first person through a Canadian girl by the name of Vivienne Michel. In an even riskier move, Bond does not come into the story until two thirds of the way through the book. While it was in many ways a brave and bold approach, it was not one that was well received by the critics. Charles Stainsby of the weekly magazine *Today* described it as 'one of the worst, most boring, badly constructed novels we have read'.

This was not the first occasion on which he had encountered bad or critical reviews relating to his plots. Having had a relatively good stretch between 1953 and 1958, *Dr. No*, published in March of that year, was accused by some critics of being a re-working of British author Sax Rohmer's *Fu Manchu*. Paul Johnson, writing in the *New Statesman*, went somewhat further by describing the book as the nastiest he had ever read. 'Mr Fleming', he wrote, 'has no literary skill; the construction of the book is chaotic, and entire incidents and situations are inserted and then forgotten in a haphazard way.' To Fleming, however, the secret of writing a best seller was not to be found in the intricacies or otherwise of the plot, it was all down to the author's ability to incentivise the reader to turn over the pages. The success of his story telling was all about how you did it rather than what you did. Nothing, in his view, should interfere with the essential dynamic of the thriller. Prose should ideally be simple and unmannered and should not linger too long over descriptive passages. Having said that, he was equally of the view that these rules were occasionally there to be broken. Looking back on the writing of *Goldfinger* in 1958, he confessed to indulging the reader with large doses of what he considered they should be interested in and proceeded to take up some three chapters in describing in fine, blow-by-blow detail, the round of golf between Goldfinger and Bond. He was equally equivocal that there should be no complications in names, relationships, journeys or geographical settings that would likely confuse or annoy the reader. Unlike Christie plots, he believed there must never be what he felt were indulgent recaps where the central character theorises in his mind on a list of suspects or reflects on what he might have done or what he proposes to do next.

Gustav Steinhauer, Melville's German intelligence opposite number and author of the Bank of England Plot, considered by many to be 'the Real Goldfinger'. *National Archive*

William Melville, the Secret Service Bureau Chief who smashed the plot to blow up the Bank of England's gold reserve in 1914. *Author's collection*

Fleming's modus operandi was to crack on at break-neck speed, hustling the reader quickly beyond what he often referred to as the 'danger points of mockery'. This approach was equally a reflection of his writing technique which embodied the principle of never correcting anything and never looking back at what he had written until he had finished.

At a time when few post-war Britons were willing or able to venture beyond their native shores on a foreign holiday, Fleming's books were the perfect antidote. His backdrops were always sunny, exciting and luxurious locations. At the same time, his narrative frequently employed the use of familiar names and objects: a Ronson lighter, a 4½-litre Bentley with an Amherst-Villiers super-charger and the Ritz Hotel in London are all points of familiarity that punctuate the reader's journey to fantastic adventure.

Ultimately, Ian's real ambition was not to be recognised as a great writer or to write great books but to see his creation James Bond make the transition to the big screen and find the success that that authors like Leslie Charteris had done. As he acknowledged himself in 1962, there was not much money to be made from book royalties and translation rights; it was selling the film rights that made it all worthwhile financially. In this sense, it is significant that when, in

1962, after some eight years of trying, he finally succeeded in obtaining a film deal with Cubby Broccoli and Harry Saltzman, the film producers found very few of his literary plots of use or value in terms of constructing scripts. Of all the Bond books he wrote, few were to make the transition from book to screen in terms of the plot.

• THE COVERS •

Fleming had done a good job as a cover designer with some of his earlier books, but when it came to *From Russia with Love* he found the best artist yet. Richard Chopping was 40 and established as a painter of exquisite flowers, plants and insects. After an exhibition of his in 1957, he and his partner Denis Wirth-Miller gave a dinner party. Francis Bacon brought Anne Fleming. Soon afterwards they and Bacon were invited to dine with the Flemings in their house in Victoria Square, a quiet enclave off the Buckingham Palace Road. Fleming, presumably having heard about Chopping's work from Anne, asked him to paint a picture he could use as the cover for his next book. (According to Chopping himself later, he was the second choice, although the first would have produced the goods even more slowly.) Money wasn't mentioned. Ian was unfairly self-deprecating about the books themselves ('You don't want to read them. They're rubbish.') For *From Russia with Love*, they agreed on a still life with gun, which Fleming would provide, and thorny rose, on a pale wood-grain background.

Chopping painted this but delivered it somewhat late, at Fleming's office in Gray's Inn Road. Fleming grinned as he entered; he was on the phone to somebody. 'You can ask him yourself,' he laughed, 'he's just walked through the door.' Chopping found himself talking to Scotland Yard. Three people had met a sudden end from the barrel of a Smith and Wesson revolver. The only licensed Smith and Wesson revolver, in the area they were searching, was the pistol Ian had given him to paint. Ian had borrowed it from a reputable gun dealer. The prime suspect, until forensics fortunately established that this gun hadn't been fired, was either Chopping, Fleming or the dealer.

Ian loved the picture. The usual rate for a book jacket was ten guineas (£10.50) but Chopping asked £30. Ian insisted he was worth £40. Chopping did a few more covers after that, and then in 1961, he began to supplement his income with a lecturing job at the Royal College of Art. He wanted to reserve his spare time for his own work. He was bored by James Bond by then anyway, and refused a fourth commission. However,

Fleming 'insisted, saying "your covers sell the books" although this had previously been hotly denied when I sought to raise my price'.

So Chopping asked for copyright, as well as much more money, and that was agreed. He then asked for royalties and was refused. So he simply put the price up with each successive job, until finally – having been paid £365 for one of them – he was publicised as 'the highest paid book jacket designer in the world'.

· 10 ·

LOVE AND MARRIAGE

• MARRIAGE •

Ian Fleming was unsuited to marriage. He was too moody, too selfish and too easily bored. The liaison with Anne, which began in the 1930s, had endured for a remarkably long time partly because they both had other relationships and other interests to pursue. They did not have to share the same roof for months on end. Sometimes they had to communicate by letter or not at all. They both delighted in sado-masochistic sex, which kept the candle burning, but inventiveness would eventually run out there too.

Once they were married they did their best to avoid passion-killing domesticity. Ian wanted to remain fit and attractive. When Barbara Skelton saw him in 1954 she noticed he no longer was; these days he had a complexion like raw beef and a big behind. Yet Ian's view, according to Bryce, was that a healthy man in his forties should be made of 'velvet stretched on bone' or turn into a middle-aged slob. Aware of increasing flab, he and Ivar agreed that they would both lose it under medical supervision within six months. Each bet the other $10,000 that he couldn't do it. If they both failed, the $20,000 would go to charity. They both succeeded. Later on, Ian did 'a champagne cure for chronic alcoholism which I find is very beneficial and my smoking has been vastly reduced, so I hope that before long a new Fleming will arise from the ashes of the old'.

He never felt good enough, or excited enough, for very long. Marriage had motivated him to stick to a routine for a purpose, but it didn't offer a thrilling life.

He was pleased to have a son, but not particularly interested. Film, TV and serial rights in the Bond books were put in trust for Caspar, but hands-on parenthood offered few delights to either Ian or Anne. Nanny Sillick looked after little Caspar at No. 16 Victoria Square and at their house in St Margaret's Bay, on the Kent coast. Permanent domestic staff were also in residence in London, which – since both Caspar's parents were often away – made him the baby boss of his own household. He had been born to parents aged

43 and 38, whose own parents would have expected the children to be 'brought down' for an hour in the early evening, and otherwise kept out of sight. So it was for Caspar in the 1950s. Nanny Sillick did the nappy changing and playing with wood bricks, the maid did the laundry, the cook mashed the baby food. After a while the Flemings decided that Nanny Sillick might as well keep Caspar down in Kent all the time, and they would visit at weekends and at Christmas. Christmas at St Margaret's Bay involved quite a lot of entertaining, so they rented the house next door for a cook. Given James Bond's fussiness over drinks and cigarettes, guests might have expected superb cuisine. Barbara Skelton, who was a good cook, found their food dreary in the extreme. When she was still married, just about, to Cyril Connolly, Connolly called her after a meal at the Flemings'.

'"What did you have to eat?" I asked, knowing the form.

'"Unripe avocados and some rather dull little soles."'

Avocados were barely known then, and only Harrods or Fortnums would stock them. Anne and Ian knew the kind of thing they should eat to look smart, but Ian at least was a steak-and-chips sort of person.

Ian's health was an ongoing concern. By the time he was 50, in 1958, he was in terrible shape. He was often drunk. He had a bad back, dodgy kidneys, a dicky heart and stress. He smoked as much as ever. When he was in Jamaica that year he kept asking Anne, by letter, to find them a house where they could settle down. He wanted a place, he said, where he could afford the heating bills. (The soul of Granny K lived on.) Anne's solution was a forty-roomed wreck in Dorset, with dry rot and a ballroom. They bought it, and it kept her conveniently occupied for the next four years. Dredging the lake cost quite a lot. When it was finished he decided to take a flat of his own at Sandwich, to be nearer the golf course.

Holidays, at least, were chosen by Ian, for Ian. In a repeat of the Esmond-Anne-Ian trip to Cornwall, he was hoping somehow to re-live happier, more innocent times. He loved fast cars and had enjoyed Kitzbühel thirty years ago, so in mid-1950s he drove Anne and Caspar to Austria in his Thunderbird in summer. There was a golf club, so he played golf. Anne painted. Presumably Nanny Sillick spent her days with the little boy. When Caspar was 7 or 8, he had a governess, who would accompany them on holiday and to Jamaica and give him the kind of attention that his parents were too self-absorbed to offer. At 10, in 1962, Caspar had a companion: his cousin Francis. Anne's sister, who like Eve Fleming's brothers was unable to manage life, died of drink that year, leaving Francis motherless. Anne more or less took him in as a companion for Caspar. It was probably too late. Anne herself was by that time addicted to barbiturates, which Caspar started taking occasionally when he was 11.

In 1960, they went to Kitbühel in winter but Ian couldn't ski. He could hardly breathe. His circulation was suffering, his heart and lungs weak. The marriage was awful. He was nasty when he was miserable and there were arguments about Goldeneye. Anne wanted him to sell it.

She had a reason: Blanche Blackwell.

• LOVE •

In 1956 Ian had met his fantasy woman. She was not in her 30s – she was only four years younger than he was – but she was the soul-mate he knew he wanted: a kind, smart, independently wealthy Jewish divorcée with an exotic heritage. She had been born in Costa Rica into one of Jamaica's oldest plantation families, the Lindos, and had married a Blackwell, related to Ian's friend John Blackwell, from the family who ran Crosse and Blackwell.

She had one son, Christopher. Her home was in Jamaica, but because Chris had been until recently at Harrow, she had spent the past several years in England. She had inherited thousands of acres of land on the island, including the part she sold to Noël Coward. Ian knew her brother, and he had been told by various people that she was an interesting woman, likeable and self-assured. There had been an affair with Errol Flynn, who had wanted to marry her.

When they met for the first time, at a social gathering, she found Fleming dreadful. She happened to mention that the area where she lived was becoming the latest gay hangout, and he said, 'Don't tell me you're a lesbian then.' He called her, in conversation with someone else, a stupid bitch.

Somehow, in spite of his insulting behaviour, they got together in the winter of 1956. Anne at the time was in England, in rehab at a health farm. She needed to stop taking the tablets. She was also avoiding Jamaica, where the Spartan facilities and irritable, preoccupied husband had become a strain. So Ian and Blanche were free to shop together for toys that Caspar could play with when he came to Jamaica next year. They were both invited to Noël Coward's house. Blanche swam like a fish. Everyone could see that she and Ian were flirting. And pretty soon, they were always invited to the same parties.

A photograph of them together on the beach shows that they were both running to fat, but they look happy. She was much better at managing him than Anne was and less insistent on being noticed. Later, as his health worsened, somebody remarked that she was exactly what he needed – a nanny.

As Christmas approached, both Ian and Anne were in England. At home Sir Anthony Eden was prime minister, but in October and early November the uproar over Suez – his disastrous attempt, with French and Israeli collaboration, to get rid of the socialist President Nasser of Egypt – left him facing fury in the House of Commons. He and his wife Clarissa required privacy, so they rented Goldeneye for a few weeks after the ceasefire of 7 November.

In theory, the governor of Jamaica's wife would arrange that they were properly catered for. In the event, it was the governor's wife and Blanche Blackwell who organised everything, and Ian's local attorney, Lahoud, who acted as liaison with the prime minister's party. The Edens were delighted with the place; it had the peace and quiet and warmth they needed and was miles from everyone they knew. Sir Anthony Eden had liver trouble caused by a botched operation, and there had been a series of operations that never seemed to help. What was not well known that he had been prescribed the sedative and stimulant drug drinamyl, against anxiety. It can affect judgement.

With the Edens quietly relaxing at Goldeneye, behind the scenes Lahoud was not reconciled to Blanche. And then he made a naïve error; one morning he told the press that the prime minister wasn't feeling very well. This of course had massive repercussions everywhere from London's political party machines to stock exchanges in London and New York. Lady Eden was absolutely furious and got rid of him, but it was too late; in London Macmillan and Butler were already jockeying for position as the man who would take over from Eden. Macmillan did, about six weeks later.

There was another, personal outcome when they got home. Clarissa mentioned to Anne, a friend of theirs, how wonderfully helpful Blanche Blackwell had been in getting Goldeneye ready for their visit.

This was devastating. As far as Anne knew, Blanche Blackwell had never set foot in Goldeneye. Ian must have been seeing her. The following year, when she got there with her older son Raymond O'Neill and saw the comforts, still in place, that had been provided in preparation for the Edens, she was deeply wounded. Ian had never allowed her to improve

Goldeneye. Blanche Blackwell was part of his life and he didn't deny it; she could perhaps have borne that, had Blanche not visibly exercised more power over her husband than she had. Power was important to Anne.

Blanche understood Ian's need for solitude. Anne, above all a social being, was impatient and annoyingly intrusive when he was writing. In 1958, Anne didn't go to Goldeneye at all. This was a huge relief. Had she done so, she would have demanded attention.

Instead Blanche was there, but only if required. She kept away during Ian's working hours, and when Hugh Pitman and his family came for a couple of weeks she took them off his hands.

• ESTRANGEMENT •

Now that Anne was aware of Blanche, there would be no reconciliation. She was humiliated but not necessarily sad. Even before Caspar was born, she had said that with Ian, 'the deserts of pomposity between the acres of wit are too vast'. She called him Thunderbird when she wrote to Evelyn Waugh, and could never be bothered to read the books. As to Ian, he found her Caesarian scars sexually off-putting and her overwhelming presence sometimes an embarrassment.

They stayed in the marriage for Caspar's sake. Holidays were increasingly taken separately. Ian spent several summers with the Bryces at Black Hole Hollow Farm, on the Vermont border, which he loved. Anne couldn't stand Ivar Bryce; she thought he was a crook. Ian, for his part, disliked Lady Diana Cooper, who was a great friend of Anne's. By the end of 1957, Ian and Anne were destroying one another and forever sniping, even in public. He accused her of constantly nagging and complaining. They decided to split up for the winter and she resorted to rehab again.

In May 1958 he would be 50. They took a second honeymoon in Venice. She walked around the galleries. He never willingly contemplated art or objects unless the subject might be of use to him. He read instead, always with a drink to hand. He drove very fast without stopping. They really had nothing in common. After Venice, Nice; he was seeing people there about filming the Bond books and had to go on to New York City afterwards for discussions. Anne was left behind.

Later on that year the Flemings were in Austria when the Gaitskells turned up. They were Hugh Gaitskell, then leader of the Labour Party, and his wife. Anne was already, unfathomably, having an affair with Hugh Gaitskell.

Ian had designed James Bond with film-making always at the back of his mind and now the books were attracting interest. Film and TV producers were nibbling. Anne went on the attack. Ian was employing lawyers here there and everywhere to deal with these things, and others, while Arnold Goodman could do it all. Ian was selfish and whatever he wanted, he got; she never got the chance to choose where they were going on holiday. And why did he have to eat so much when it was making him fat? He usually said something spiteful in return.

Beneath it all, he felt desperately tired of James Bond. He felt he had used all the situations and characters he had absorbed as material during the war. All that remained now was to find exotic locations for improbable plots. His heart wasn't in it anymore; yet there was nothing else; he had become the Writer, Ian Fleming. When Bryce talked about writing a book he wrote to him:

You will be constantly depressed by the progress of the opus and feel it is all nonsense and that nobody will be interested. These are the moments when you must all the more obstinately stick to your schedule and do your daily stint …

It would be worth it, he thought, if he could find somebody to produce Bond as a film. Hollywood was a writer's only chance of making enough to retire on.

· 11 ·

THE BIG MISTAKE

· NOT THE SAME THING ·

The second, third and subsequent Bond books hit the stores in the spring of every year. Ian felt he was on a treadmill, but one he could not afford to fall off. It was true that with every new book his readership increased; still, the revenue from books alone was not even in the same league as the revenue from movie distribution and TV series. The trouble was that a one hour TV show had already been made, with his blessing, in America and it hadn't worked at all. The director had swept the British settings and characters under the carpet because a British agent would never work in Middle America.

A James Bond film would be better, but it must have a British star. As soon as you started talking that way to US producers they pulled their offer off the table.

So this went on, this hoping, and blundering, for several years. Ian did not know any dedicated script agents or big directors. He would try to work on a film proposal sometimes then put it down again. He didn't altogether know how to do this or whom to send it to; he had no inside knowledge of the film industry. Would-be developers came to him and they faded away, usually, or optioned a book and then did nothing with it.

This went on intermittently until, in 1959, Ivar Bryce came to the rescue.

The year before, Bryce had set up a film production company with an Irishman in his early 30s called Kevin McClory. McClory, after a personally devastating war, had worked his way up the film industry from runner through boom operator to assistant director and finally, second unit director. Both John Huston and Mike Todd found him reliable and passionate about the work. They liked him and kept in touch. And he was creative. Wide-screen films were the new big thing in the 1950s, and McClory had an idea for a story featuring scenes shot underwater in Todd-AO. He interested John Steinbeck in

Kevin McClory, the man who claimed to have created the 'big screen' James Bond. *Philadelphia Enquirer*

contributing a treatment for it, but it fizzled out. By that time McClory had another idea, derived from a short story about a boy who runs away from home to live in the Golden Gate Bridge.

For this one, he raised seed money and production funding to shoot a film set in London and Tower Bridge. McClory contributed his expertise in the film industry – he would be producer/director – and Bryce supplied the money. Together they formed Xanadu Productions in London. Bryce benefited from Ernie Cuneo's legal advice. McClory went over budget, but he made *The Boy and the Bridge*, and it was chosen as the British entry for the 1959 Venice Biennale.

Fleming saw the film, was impressed and started talking to both of them about investing in a Bond movie, which he would write and Kevin would direct and produce. 'There's no-one who I would prefer to produce James Bond for the screen', he wrote to Kevin after seeing his work. He probably, at the time, didn't know the difference between a producer and a director and was using the verb loosely.

Anyhow while Kevin was busy promoting *The Boy and the Bridge* all over Europe and Hollywood, backed by Bryce's investment, Ian began work on a treatment for a Bond film. Kevin had told him that the Bond stories, as they stood, were not suitable. They would need a fresh approach for a medium that relied on vision and sound alone, and the sadism would have to go. The neatest solution was an entirely new story, specially written for the screen, using underwater locations in the Bahamas. Bryce, Kevin McCory and Cuneo talked about possible plotlines early in 1959; Cuneo hurriedly put the essentials into a memo and sent it off to Fleming.

Fleming expressed satisfaction. The first Bond film would be a fast-moving caper involving an atom bomb, an enemy agent infiltrating a troupe of wartime entertainers – Noël Coward and Laurence Olivier in cameo roles – a female CIA spy for love interest, and an underwater battle with scuba divers.

Ian loved it, especially the underwater idea. There was some urgency about getting this right, though. Fleming was a loyal friend to Bryce, and he and Bryce agreed that Xanadu should always have first option on making James Bond films, but at least four other offers were on the table and Fleming's agent at MCA was pushing him to make a decision. Fleming and Bryce were communicating by letter. Fleming needed to be part of Xanadu. Bryce stuffed his mouth with gold: a cheque for $50,000 dollars at once, to spend on buying shares in the new, Nassau-based version of Xanadu. Fleming then wrote to him including what he called 'the legal bit':

... in exchange for $50,000 dollars' worth of shares
in the new company, I give you the right to make the
first full length James Bond feature film. I will write
a full suggested treatment which you can alter as you
wish and I will provide editorial and advisory services whenever they can be helpful.

Almost as soon as he'd written to Bryce, he started
having second thoughts. He told his MCA agent in
London what he'd done; then he wrote again to say
he was with Xanadu now so he wouldn't need MCA
again. His agent mildly replied pointing out that he
was now potentially tied into an agreement with
Xanadu which – if their 'first full length James Bond
feature film' never got made – would stymie other
offers for good, and since he had been paid by shares
in something that depended for its success on his own
labour, it didn't look like such a great deal.

Ian stayed with MCA and got on with the treatment. There was some to-and-fro over exactly who
the antagonists were – Communists had been the
original idea, then SPECTRE was invented, but should
it be Mafia? Discussions went on, and problems were
resolved, long-distance. But whatever solutions were
found, and however hard Ian tried, constructing the
thing was agony. He discovered that a novel and a film

are not the same thing. He didn't know how a script worked. In his books, key points were explained in imaginary internal monologues by Bond. There would be a slow build. Readers would see the action, and learn the backstory, from Bond's point of view. Ian tried to carry that into film, with plenty of spectacular scenes, but the result was clunky. McClory must have groaned when he saw it. A dull start was followed by static scenes of dialogue between static people, gimmicky effects, sadistic torture, cardboard characters and holes in the plot which, to pass unnoticed, would require impossible elisions between scenes.

They needed a screenwriter.

• FINDING A WRITER •

Kevin McClory was firmly in favour of finding a specialist writer. Ian willingly agreed but was anxious that it must be a British one; he did not want a repeat of the American gumshoe clichés that had ruined the TV show in 1954. They all favoured a British cast and crew as well for economic reasons. If the locations were in the Bahamas (where Kevin had found just the right place to build a couple of sound stages), and the actors, writer, producer, director and most of the crew were Brits as well, the James Bond film would qualify for the Eady Levy, a financial advantage designed to promote British film.

Paul Dehn was approached to write the script and declined. He had seen the treatment. There wasn't sufficient scope for character development, and in any case, he had already worked on a similar, successful film that involved the theft of an atom bomb; helpfully, he suggested a change in its construction. But he wouldn't be writing it.

They were halfway to hiring someone called Fairchild before they recognised that he would be out of his depth – probably literally. They learned that Fairchild had avoided engaging with underwater scenes in a similar project. They kept looking.

McClory's dismayed reaction to Ian's script may have hurt. He was less charmed by what he called McClory's 'blarney' than Bryce was, and as his communications with Bryce grew chummier, he fell to implicit criticism of McClory. Bryce himself was annoyed with McClory by then. Kevin was still spending Xanadu money on the festival circuit while *The Boy on the Bridge* had not yet found a distributor. Kevin seemed as confident as ever, although privately he must have been disappointed. Before he met Bryce, he had discussed both his underwater film project and the Bridge one with Mike Todd, who had advised him to go with the undersea film. *The Boy on the Bridge*, he said, would win a lot of awards but 'you can't eat awards'. He had been right.

Nonetheless McClory remained fully engaged with the Bond project, promising jobs to good people – pending a good script.

In letters to Bryce, Fleming questioned Kevin's saleability as director. He had been told, rightly, that distributors liked big name stars and big name directors. Maybe, he suggested, they should ask Hitchcock. Hitchcock, they were warned, would take the whole thing over: he would bring in his own team, writers, everybody.

While these discussions were going on, they still hadn't fully set up Xanadu in Nassau (as opposed to Xanadu, London, which was a partnership between Bryce and McClory). They lined up a couple of mon-eyed investors, but they needed to work out what part everyone was playing. As Fleming saw it, Kevin should have no particular role. He was rather too small-time for such a big project; he hadn't got the track record as director that was required and as to money, he was not a professional producer. Could he in fact account for what he was spending already?

Kevin knew nothing of this Nassau company. Bryce asked him for a breakdown of the money he was spending. At this point, Kevin thought he was equal partner with Bryce in Xanadu, that it had first option on the Bond film, and that his input into that was considerable. He had been drawing up a production team, looking for a writer, even getting storyboards done by John Huston's artist. Under the original agreement, he would work on it for a salary and expenses and have an equal share of the profits. Nothing had been said to him to indicate that another director, far less another producer, would be sought. There was ill feeling. Bryce was difficult about the salary Kevin felt was due to him. He wanted to know where the money was going. Kevin told him the accounts had been filed with the accountant and were there to be seen.

Ian and his various agents and lawyers were still fielding other offers for James Bond from film and television. Harry Saltzman, who would later meet Cubby Broccoli and make seriously profitable movies out of Bond, had an option on two of the books. In the meantime Bryce and Xanadu were in the doldrums, largely caused by Ian quietly undermining Kevin McClory and Ian and Bryce believing that 'gentlemen's agreements' were an adequate substitute for legal documents.

At this point, in the autumn of 1959, McClory found Jack Whittingham.

Whittingham was perfect: he had been a journalist and a screenwriter since the war, had excellent credits and, best of all, Ian liked him a lot. He immediately suggested improvements to the treatment. His agent negotiated a deal, and McClory, Whittingham and Fleming got together to work on developing a script. Notes would be made at script conferences and Whittingham would go away and make at couple of drafts, at least, before the final shooting script. The general idea – atomic bomb theft, blackmail of world powers, underwater scenes – was pretty much what it had always been but thanks to professional input it would move faster and be more credible.

Fleming attended about four of these meetings, and he registered the title *Thunderball*, before disappearing to Jamaica to write his new book. Bryce was anxious about money and progress and demanded from McClory 'my script in my hand' by February 1960, about six weeks away. This seemed odd to McClory, who had understood that they were partners but now increasingly felt he was being pushed out; even more so when it was Cuneo, the lawyer, who started to ring on the subject of money – and was getting nasty.

THE KILLER

· GOLDENEYE ·

The tenor of conversations between Bryce and McClory had become impossible. Once the script was delivered, McClory knew he was out. Bryce intimated that there was going to be a new company and although he would be happy to offer McClory a position such as associate producer, Kevin himself did not necessarily hold any rights in the script. McClory hadn't managed to find any backers (McClory showed that he had). McClory had spent money like water (McClory protested that every penny was accounted for). McClory was also furious because he knew Bryce, or Cuneo or both, were making possibly slanderous remarks about his use of Xanadu's funds.

Also because – despite having asked for some input from Fleming – he hadn't heard a word.

McClory decided to visit Fleming in Jamaica. He made sure that the script, which had been much refined and improved from the preliminary screen treatment that Fleming had seen, with lots of new twists, was in Fleming's hands in advance of his own arrival in Jamaica and that Fleming would know where to find him.

When he was, after several days of silence, invited to Goldeneye, Fleming told him that he hadn't read the script. In any case, he asked, what qualifications did McClory have to produce the film? McClory was astonished. What did that mean?

'Well, what have you done, old boy?'

McClory told him. Fleming said this was now a big production. McClory agreed that it would be, thanks to his work. He said it was a $3 million picture and he could raise the money.

He left knowing that Fleming did not want to work with him and Bryce was evading confrontation. In March, Bryce gave him six more months to come up with production money from one of the big studios, but it was all a sham. McClory read in the papers, in 1960, that *Casino Royale* was about to go into production thanks to a deal with Fox. So much for the 'first' James Bond film being the property of his partnership with Bryce.

• 'It's Different' •

When Fleming submitted his manuscript of *Thunderball* that summer, his publishers were pleased with it and certainly relieved. For the past few years Ian had been complaining about the difficulty of coming up with new stuff for Bond to do, and reaction to *The Spy Who Loved Me* had been awful. A senior editor wrote to say that *Thunderball* worked particularly well because the more outrageously sadistic stuff had gone. It was more like life, and less like fantasy. And when it was published in hardback, and serialised in the *Daily Express*, in 1961, reviewers said the same thing; Fleming was better than before.

McClory was livid. *Thunderball* was 'by Ian Fleming', copyrighted to Glidrose, without even an 'inspired by' on the cover or the title page, far less an acknowledgement of co-authorship. But significant parts of it had originated in ideas that he and Jack Whittingham had devised and which Fleming had stolen from Whittingham's script.

McClory attempted to prevent publication with an injunction against sales. Jonathan Cape expressed shock. They hadn't known, they said, until a letter arrived from McClory's lawyers quite recently, that there was the remotest likelihood of legal action and even now, they didn't know why. The book was being advertised all over town; foreign rights were being sold, 130 review copies had been despatched and books had been delivered to booksellers. Should sales be stopped, they would suffer terrible losses.

McClory lost, in a hearing that lasted just 90 minutes.

'I'm sure Bond never had to go through anything like this,' Ian remarked with a smile to reporters as he left the court.

McClory marshalled his lawyers. They told him to forget it.

Jack Whittingham's daughter got a job, typing for a firm of solicitors. It was a big firm with a lot of famous clients, and she went home and told her dad about them. This is how McClory and Whittingham came to engage Peter Carter-Ruck. A famous libel lawyer, he had in the past won cases for people like Lord Rothermere and Winston Churchill. He thought these two men had a good case. When he sat down with McClory and Whittingham to work out just how much of the story was not Fleming's but theirs, the two texts side by side, they came up with two hundred pages of material that had been lifted or adapted from the script Ian had seen in February 1960.

Carter-Ruck and Whittingham got on well, but Whittingham had done a law degree at Oxford and knew that Law can defeat Justice. Carter-Ruck told him the chances of their winning or losing were about fifty-fifty. Whittingham could see the boxes and boxes of files and hours of investigation in this case. Money was pouring into the lawyers' coffers by the hour. If he lost, if Fleming's and Cape's costs had to be paid as well as his own, there would be no more lovely house in Surrey, no more private schools for the children. He was unwell; like Ian, he smoked and drank too much and had a weak heart. He pulled out, assigning his rights in the screenplay to Kevin. Carter-Ruck told Whittingham that if Kevin won, he would have a good chance of success in a subsequent action.

McClory stuck with it. He had married Bobo Sigrist, who was extremely rich.

Fleming, Bryce, Jonathan Cape, Mr Cuneo from New York, Farrers and Mr Harbottle from St James's Square, confabulated. In July, McClory was offered £10,000 and many other incentives to go away. McClory did not bite.

The trial was only weeks away when he and Carter-Ruck finally received the full documentation, the years of pertinent correspondence — copies of Fleming's and Xanadu's parallel arrangements with people like United Artists, Broccoli and Saltzmann, and other film and TV producers and companies; most importantly, the letters and cables between Fleming and Bryce which demonstrated intent to cut him out of the Bond film and out of the company set up to exploit it. He was advised to sue for breach of copyright, breach of confidence, conversion, breach of contract, false representation of authorship and slander of title.

The case opened at the Royal Courts of Justice in November 1963. The press were agog. The *Mail* and the *Express* alternated pictures of Anne in floor-length mink and off-the-face mink hat, alongside Ian in his suit and bow tie, with photographs of Kevin in an overcoat and his pretty wife in pillbox hat and suit, Jacquie Kennedy style.

The evidence was damning. McClory brought several witnesses from the film industry who attested to his professional competence and efforts to get the Bond film off the ground, as well as Whittingham of course who was in the best possible position to discern exactly what creative input had gone into *Thunderball*. Fleming was mortified.

On the second Friday, proceedings were suddenly adjourned just as Kevin McClory had taken the stand. Leading Counsel for both sides had separately seen the judge in his room. The court would reconvene on Monday 2 December. On the Sunday afternoon, it was all settled. McClory demanded, and got, full payment of his legal costs; film rights in *Thunderball*; copyright in the finished picture and all its scripts; and damages, in restitution for mental anguish and physical inconvenience. The damages would be £50,000, today's equivalent of which would be scores of millions.

After a 10-minute consultation the terms were agreed. Bryce would pay.

• A Sad End •

Why did Fleming and Bryce cave in? Probably because they were likely to lose a lot of money, but Robert Sellers, who wrote *The Battle for Bond*, believed that the main consideration was Ian's poor health. He had recently been told he had five years to live. He already looked extremely frail for a man of 55.

There is another slight possibility in Sellers' book, which doesn't make very good sense. It seems the letter had been handed to the judge by Bryce's QC with the words 'I think it would be unwise for me to comment on this.' The judge read it. 'All I can say is that I am very surprised to see it,' he said, and handed it back. Sellers suggests, as a 'side-note', a homosexual relationship between Ivar and Ian which came close to being expressed in letters between them. Homosexuality was illegal at the time. The inference is that McClory had produced a copy of the letter as some sort of blackmail threat and the QC wanted the judge to know.

It's a red herring. Fleming's arrogant dismissal of medical advice was finishing all the games at once. Ian was already very ill indeed, and a few weeks later, he nearly died of a heart attack. He was taken by ambulance from an editorial conference at Gray's Inn Road straight to King Edward VII Hospital, where he spent more than a month. Yet astonishingly, as he convalesced, thinking, perhaps, of happier times, he produced something completely different: *Chitty Chitty Bang Bang*.

This was Ian with a burden lifted, writing about a wonderful car he had seen as a boy at Brooklands racetrack. The real car had been driven by Count Zborowski of Higham Park, wearing a flying helmet and a big black moustache. When Ian saw the race he was enchanted. As who wouldn't be, for Zborowski was a dashing young man of fabulous wealth,

descended from the Astors, who had built a miniature railway line around Higham Park – not because
it joined up with any other railway but just for fun.
His favourite racing cars, Chitty Bang Bang and Chitty
Chitty Bang Bang, had aeroplane engines in them and
must have been quite loud. 'Never say No to adventures', a character in the story tells the children.

It was his first children's story and the publishers
accepted it at once. It must have been a great comfort, after the agonies of tedious work on James Bond,
to know that his creative years were not finished. He
could still produce a damn good yarn that people
liked reading. It took his mind off things. Caspar was
difficult. Anne was annoyed because Blanche was still
in the picture. She was angry because he'd got Chris
Blackwell a job on the set of *Dr. No*. Looking on the
bright side, Broccoli and Saltzman would bring *Dr. No*
to British screens the following year.

He had to convalesce, though. In Jamaica with
Blanche, all passion spent, he had decided to write a
book about ganja and sent away for research material.
He would not write another Bond book this year.

He would spend the late summer in Kent. With
the passing of years St Margaret's Bay attracted Ian
more and more. He liked the golf club crowd. He was
pretty special there. Anne's brother Hugo, a writer,

once invented a character based on Ian, of whom he wrote 'there was no limit, no limit at all, to his capacity for feeling inferior'. There was no chance of feeling inferior surrounded by the admiring fellows in the bar at the golf club. He was often there. *Chitty Chitty Bang Bang* would be released in October.

The worst thing, that summer, was the death of his mother. She had lived in Nassau for years with the Marquis of Winchester. He died at 99. The ultimate fate of the Marchioness is not recorded. After his death Eve decamped to Cannes where she lived at the Metropole Hotel and was driven around in a Rolls Royce. Ian had brought her back to London a few years ago, and she died in August.

He did not divorce Anne. In 1962 he told Blanche he was going to, but then he also told Anne that he wasn't seeing Blanche any more. In fact she came to England when he did, and was having lunch with him at a pleasant hotel in the Home Counties every week.

Two weeks after his mother's death, while at home in his flat in St Margaret's Bay, he suffered another major cardiac arrest. He was taken to hospital, where he died.

• AFTERWARDS •

Caspar was a continuing problem, and would die young and dissolute in 1975. Anne drank too much and died in 1981. Blanche must have been consoled by the success of her own son who in adulthood became world famous as Chris Blackwell, the music producer and founder of Island Records.

The James Bond books and *Chitty Chitty Bang Bang* are still in print. As to the films, *Chitty Chitty Bang Bang* came out in 1968 and is a perennial favourite. Fortunes have been made in the Bond film industry, which has employed a succession of stars, female leads, musicians and title designers, makers of gadgetry, special effects people, writers, producers, directors, crew and editors. Entire careers, in Britain and America, have been based on reputations made by those films. They get better and better, although perhaps less and less like any James Bond Ian Fleming imagined.

Kevin McClory was in continual litigation over *Thunderball* for over forty years. Which is probably not what he intended to happen.

How is Ian Fleming remembered? With adoration, by his fans, for inventing a British fantasy figure who lives on throughout the world.

LIST OF ABBREVIATIONS

BEF	British Expeditionary Force
BSC	British Security Co-ordination
CIA	Central Intelligence Agency
DNI	Director of Naval Intelligence
FBI	Federal Bureau of Investigation
GPU	*Gosudarstvennoye Politicheskoye Upravleniye* (Soviet Security and Intelligence Service 1922–23)
KGB	*Komitet Gosudarstvennoi Bezopastnosti* (Soviet Security and Intelligence Service 1954–91)
MCA	Music Corporation of America
MGB	*Ministerstvo Gosudarstvennoi Bezopastnosti* (Soviet Security and Intelligence Service 1943–53)

MI5	Military Intelligence 5 (aka Security Service)
MI6	Military Intelligence 6 (aka SIS)
NID	Naval Intelligence Department
NKVD	*Narodnyi Kommissariat Vnutrennikh Del* (Soviet Security and Intelligence Service 1934–43
OGPU	*Obyedinennoye Gosudarstvennoye Politicheskoye* (Soviet Security and Intelligence Service 1923–34)
OSS	Office of Strategic Services (forerunner of CIA)
POW	Prisoner of War
PWE	Political Warfare Executive
RADA	Royal Academy of Dramatic Art
RAF	Royal Air Force
RNVR	Royal Navy Volunteer Reserve
SIS	Secret Intelligence Service (aka MI6)
SMERSH	*Spetsyalnye Metody Razoblacheniya Shpyonov* (Special Methods of Spy Detection)
SPECTRE	Special Executive for Counterintelligence, Terrorism, Revenge and Extortion
USSR	Union of Soviet Socialist Republics
WO	War Office